Relationships
...Self
...Family
...God

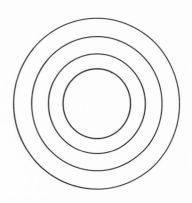

Relationships

...Self
...Family
...God

PAUL H. DUNN
and RICHARD M. EYRE

BOOKCRAFT INC.
SALT LAKE CITY, UTAH

Library of Congress Catalog Card Number: 74-75536

ISBN 0-88494-213-9

1st Printing, 1974

LITHOGRAPHED IN U.S.A.

PUBLISHERS PRESS
SALT LAKE CITY, UTAH

gift
from
C.G.

Acknowledgments

I gratefully acknowledge the great contribution of spirit and talent provided by Richard M. Eyre. His insights and understanding of gospel truths are both refreshing and appropriate. Brother Eyre's wife, Linda, has been an excellent sounding board.

Any book requires the efforts of many. My thanks to those who have constantly encouraged such efforts; and I express appreciation to my secretary, Sharene Miner, for her excellent typing and proofreading.

I am particularly indebted to my wife, Jeanne, my partner in our *eternal relationship,* for her support and constant reminder of true principles. Her life has been so characteristic of truths contained in this volume.

—*Paul H. Dunn*

I feel greatly indebted:

To Paul Dunn, who taught me so much of this so long before it was written.

To my wife Linda, who continues to show me the nature and the joy of true relationships.

To Richard Rosine, whose graphic view of life influenced this book and created the game on page 57.

—*Richard M. Eyre*

Contents

Introduction   1

PART ONE: RELATIONSHIPS WITH SELF 11
  1. Why Are You? 16
  2. Who Are You? 24
  3. Where Are You? 35
  4. How Are You? 41
  5. What Are You? 59
  6. When Are You? 72

PART TWO: RELATIONSHIPS WITH FAMILY 83
  7. The First Priority 85
  8. Oneness 102
  9. Stewardship 119

PART THREE: RELATIONSHIPS WITH GOD 145
  10. Knowing and Loving .147
  11. Asking and Listening 164
  12. Being and Returning .180

Index 193

Introduction

● First, Relationships:

People always said they could see
a certain magic
between the father and his daughter.
Even when she was just a toddler (and he just a graduate student)
there was an open, visible, two-way pride . . . .
and for sixteen years since then, it had grown . . . . his joy in
all she had learned, all she had become, and mostly
in the fact that she was *his* daughter . . . .
her joy in all he was and all he stood for, and mostly
in the fact that he was *her* daddy.
(And that was still his name,
because she still felt the same simple love and
respect
that she had when "Daddy" was the first
and only
word she could say.)
Between them, a total openness and love and trust
      had developed . . . .
so complete that facades and competition and the need to prove
had never even flickered into the relationship . . . .
and such a oneness that the sharing of a happy memory
stirred more joy
than the original event,
and the sharing of troubles came as second nature.

She knew things about herself when she was with him
that she didn't know when she was alone . . . .
and so did he.

Long walks happened between them now . . . .
sometimes for reasons, sometimes for none, and brought about
a communication so complete
that both felt a lingering awareness of a *third* present entity . . . .
a clarifying catalystic force
that transcended the words they spoke
and telegraphed feelings,
heart to heart.

One clear soft evening
in autumn,
beneath the lofting elms that shrouded their street,
she slipped her hand into his and whispered above the stillness,
"Daddy . . . . what is the most important thing of all?"
It was a silly question in a way . . . . a profound one in another . . . .
She knew it was . . . . but it was a night for questions
     like that . . . .
they had time.

The father thought as they walked,
for several silent minutes,
and then he gave his daughter the right answer
in one word:
"Relationships."

The thought had never come to him like that before,
yet as he said it, he knew it had a kind of inspiration
and his mind formulated questions to teach his daughter
what he felt.

"Can you think of a single better measurement of happiness
than the number and depth of the relationships
a person has?"
The moonlight caught her hair as her head turned,
"Certainly not money . . . . not possessions . . . . maybe testimony
and conviction that God lives . . . .
but that *is* a relationship, isn't it . . . .
with God?"
His thoughts rushed to catch hers,
"What is that relationship . . . . with God . . . . what is its nature?"
"Parent-Child."
"You know, we say it so often . . . . I wonder if we really hear it.
Does the phrase 'I am a child of God' stop in your mind
as it goes through your ears?
And how many do you think really believe the phrase . . . .
(Assuming that understanding it is prerequisite to believing it)?"
"Not many, Daddy . . . .
if we did
we would spend more *time* seeking to strengthen and improve that
one relationship."

He nodded, then went on, teaching himself as he taught her . . . .
"Is there anything you can take with you . . . . from this life
to the next

other than the relationships you have formed?"
She paused for some time . . . . formulating what she thought was
a full answer,
"To be able to retain our relationships beyond this earth
must be our greatest blessing . . . .
but there *is* more that we can take . . . .
Knowledge, judgment, capacities . . . . all that we become
internally
while we are here."
They walked on in silence for a few moments and then
her definition of "relationships" expanded to match his
and she went on,
"Relationships with *self* . . . . that's what all of these things are."

From that plateau, he reached again,
"Is there anything else? I mean
if a person was suddenly voided of all the relationships he had . . . .
would there be anything left?"
"No . . . . nothing . . . .
except maybe the potential to build new relationships."

Now their thoughts leap-frogged past each others'.
Her answers went beyond his questions and bounced his mind
into deeper perspectives.
"Can't almost everything be translated into a relationship . . . .
our problems,
our fulfillments,
our concerns and worries, our joys and pleasures . . . .

don't all stem from one relationship or another . . . .
and if they do, why don't we focus more effort
on relationships?"
"I don't know, Daddy . . . . I guess partly because we all work
so hard on achievement . . . .
on getting *things* done and on gaining material things.
That word is really the villain, isn't it? . . . . "Things" . . . .
things are the antithesis of people;
and that's the choice we face so often . . . .
people or things . . . .
relationships or achievements . . . .
taking time to get to know someone or getting another thing done.
Why is it that we usually choose the thing over the person,
even when we know that the thing is temporary
and the person is forever?"
Now he was answering instead of asking,
"Maybe . . . .
maybe because we think of relationships not as ends in themselves
but as the means to other ends.
When you think about it, our 'relating' usually takes one
of two forms . . . .
either it is small talk, for social reasons,
with no motives;
or it has ulterior motives of achieving some objective . . . .
some *thing* other than the relationship itself."

"Daddy, how many real relationships do you have? And
how many
do you need?"

"I don't know . . . . I mean, I guess that
it depends on what a real relationship is.
What constitutes one . . . . what are the essential ingredients?
What do we mean when we say
'a real relationship'?"
So they built a mental list as their walking rustled the leaves
underfoot.
First the father, then the daughter . . . .
stimulating each other's thought . . . .
setting up an expanded definition of an ideal relationship
and of what it would contain:

Investment of time . . . . together
Trust
Openness
Honesty - Integrity
Shared experiences
Background knowledge
Personality insight
Respect
Interest
Concern
Admiration
Commonality
Commitment
Giving of one's self
Empathy
Understanding
Communication

Patience
Love
Sincerity
Delight
Participation
Challenge
Stimulation
Progression
Tolerance
Listening
Receiving
Sharing
.

Finally, a longer silence signaled that the list
was done,
at least for then.
They had walked a mile, the moon was higher . . . .
"Can you imagine the value of one relationship possessing all
these qualities?
Can you even compare it with anything else?"

The conversation shifted from question and answer
to question and question
because
some questions needed no verbal answers
and others needed reflection and pondering beyond that one
crisp evening:
"How many of the 'relationship components' in the list
apply to a relationship with God?

to a relationship with family?
to a relationship with self?"
"How many real relationships do
you
have . . . . (if the list is your criteria)?
How many *should* you have . . . . (if 'should' is defined as
'prerequisite to happiness')?
How many do you *need* . . . . (if 'need' is defined as
'essential to exaltation')?"
"Is a deep relationship selfish
or selfless?
or both?"
"Is there anything more exciting
than really relating to someone?
Is there any thrill
to match?"

(Her hand tightened on his fingers, and *performed* the answer
to the last question.)

They turned for home
but the talk continued on that and other nights . . . .
and focused
on Relationships with Self
Relationships with God
Relationships with Family . . . .
for they are the three that are essential
to exaltation

And they are the three on which the full Gospel sheds
so much
unique and additional light.

● Now some introductory comments regarding this book:

The *style*
is short and terse.
What we need is not more speed readers,
but fewer superfluous words.
You add your own adjectives and applications
and then
it will be your book,
and not ours.

The *intended readership*
is not youth or adult, but both . . . .
because the nature of the topic
is such
that no one has achieved it fully. . . .
and everyone needs it dearly.

The *reading*
of this book, to be meaningful,
requires as much inspiration as the writing.
(Just as the listener must be inspired to get the full impact
of an inspired talk.)
If you will read with the higher-realm consciousness
of the Spirit,
then you will understand the essential relationships of your life
far beyond the point to which the simple words
of this book
can take you.

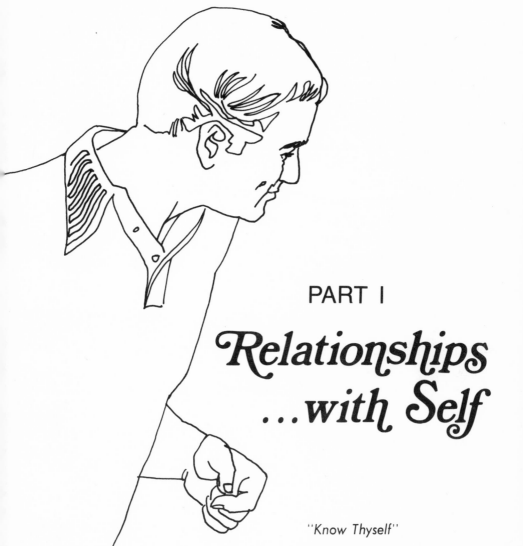

PART I

Relationships
...with Self

"Know Thyself"

● Relationships with self . . . .
two questions:
1. Isn't the whole notion of a "relationship with self"
a misnomer . . . . a paradox?
How does someone relate to himself? Doesn't it take
two
to relate?
2. Why start there? Is it more important
than relationships with family or with God?

Two answers:
1. "You" are plural . . . .
made up of spiritual, emotional, physical, mental and social
selves,
and each
relates to the others . . . .
Furthermore, if "relationship" implies "knowing,"
then relationships with self means the knowing of self . . . .
which all men need.
2. You could say,
"Until you have a relationship with yourself, you can't really
have one with anyone else . . . . "
The trouble is that you could also say,
"Until you have a relationship with someone else, you can't really
have one with yourself . . . . "

A relationship with God, a relationship with self,
a relationship with another person . . . .
none
can fully exist independently.
Each feeds on the other . . . . and they do not come
in any kind of set, sequential
order.
So . . . .
"Relationships with Self" is not first because it
necessarily *comes* first,
but because it can best be *discussed* first . . . .
since its discussion forms parameters and lays foundations
for the discussion of other relationships.

With Self   **15**

This first part asks the reader why he is,
who he is,
where he is,
how he is,
what he is,
and when he is.
The why and the who are *background.*
(Their answers are known.)
The where and how are *evaluation.*
(Their answers must be furnished by the reader.)
The what and when are *resolution.*
(Their answers are whatever the reader makes them.)

The objectives here
are to *teach you* who you are and why you are . . . .
to help you *discover* where you are and how you are . . . . and
to help you *determine* what you are and when you are . . . .
and to *prove* to you that all of the
"relationship components" in the introduction
apply
to your relationship with yourself.

Chapter 1

Why Are You?

- A train lurched,
  A man slipped, hit his head, blacked out . . . .
  awoke with amnesia.
  1. Who am I?
  2. Where did I come from?
  3. Why am I here?
  4. Where am I going?
  The conductor could only guess on number four . . . .
  couldn't even do that
  on the other three.

We all experienced a kind of spiritual amnesia when we were born.
Most churches only guess at number four . . . .
They say . . . . "heaven or hell."
And the "answers" they give for the other three are all the same:
"We can't know . . . . that's the beauty of it."

But we *must* know . . . .
else what eternal reason
for riding at all
and what possibility of knowing ourselves?

The answers, when they *are* known,
are simple,
yet they have such remarkable impact
that our faculties
are seldom aroused enough to fully receive them.

1. A child of God.
2. From a pre-existence with God.
3. To become more like God.
4. To return to God.

Now magnify those answers a little more:
1. A spirit son or daughter
begotten by a Heavenly Father . . . .
2. In a pre-existence
where we helped to determine and plan our own progress . . . .
3. And decided to come to this earth
to gain physical bodies and to be tested . . . .
4. And thus to develop the capacities that make us more like God,
and that allow us to return to His presence
and to progress further.

Now turn the microscope to a still higher power:
1. The literal offspring of a personal and loving
Heavenly Father
who created spiritual bodies for our intelligences . . . .
2. Intelligences who had existed from the beginning with God,
and who became God's spirit children and
participated
in a great debate regarding the ground rules for this
physical existence;
and chose a plan of free agency
over one of coercion . . . .
3. And thus came to this earth
to exercise that free will and to learn faith, discipline
    and discernment

as facilitated by a physical body and by lack of memory
of our pre-earthly existence . . . .
4. Thus to prove ourselves worthy and capable
of returning
to God
and of progressing on to still another stage in a process of
eternal progression.

These are *answers* . . . .
answers which can simplify and clarify and solidify
our lives
if we can but grasp them
and understand them.

You are the same entity, the same intelligence, the same being
now
that you were in the pre-existence . . . .
with rough edges, with inadequacies
that need perfecting.
And this life is the time to discover your potentials,
to learn the discipline that can govern
the goal-striving mechanism of your body and mind . . . .
and to learn the principle of faith . . . . to pass through the doors
of spiritual enlightenment and insight
that faith can open.

• Scientists have discovered 7×10^{13} stars . . . .
  How many is that?
  If each were a single piece of paper,
  stood up and pressed flat against the next,
  7×10^{13} would stretch around the world
  six hundred times.
  Each star is a sun . . . . with planets revolving around it.
  Our sun is a *small* star . . . .
  one of 7×10^{13}.
  And you are one small speck on one small planet
  revolving around one small sun.
  Pretty small?
  Yes.
  But consider this . . . .
  When you look at the night sky, and see the vast immensity
  of stars and space,
  you are looking at the *handiwork* of God.
  When you look at another person (or in the mirror),
  you are looking at the *literal offspring of God*
  for whom all that handiwork
  was made.

  "Confident humility."
  A contradiction in terms? Are they opposites?
  No, because
  Humility is an understanding of your relationship to God,
  and that relationship
  is parent-child . . . .

What could inspire more confidence than that?
Therefore, one can possess the two simultaneously:
Humility . . . . in recognition of the greatness of God
in contrast with our own "beginner's status" . . . .
Simultaneous confidence in ourselves as His children . . . . and
(because of that noble heritage)
as possessors of ultimate and infinite potential.

Psychiatry and psychology ask the right questions . . . .
Who are you? and why are you? . . . .
But they may look in the wrong place for the answers. They look
inside . . . .
in us . . . .
instead of outside, from God.
Self-image psychology tries to piece together some
        positive concepts,
but it lacks the very basis for that image,
which is a knowledge of our origins
and heritage.

Envision the supposed orphan who discovers that he is the son
of the King . . . .
beggar turned Prince . . . .
and the change is more mental than material.
So why not we
when we understand and thus truly discover
our eternal and personal relationship
to the Creator of this earth, our Elder Brother,
and to His Father,
our Father.

And this special confidence comes not only from the
cerebral knowledge
that we are God's children,
but from the Holy Ghost
who tells us in our minds and in our hearts[1]
so that our confidence waxes strong.[2]

We often hear,
"Where much is given, much is expected,"
and we assume that the first "much" means material . . . .
More so, it means knowledge of our origins, our purpose,
        our destiny;
and as much more should be expected of those who have
        this knowledge
as the next man on the train
who didn't bump his head . . . .
because the advantages of knowing
are fantastic.

Our identity, our destiny, our origins, our purpose . . . .
The scriptures really do tell of all four.
Take a look at the chart on the next page . . . . look at the
basic questions and their basic answers,
and as you look, remember
that each answer can be just as
surface and meaningless
or as
deep and meaningful
as your spirit cares to make it.

---

[1]Doctrine and Covenants 8:1-3.
[2]Doctrine and Covenants 121:45.

Relationships

22

1 WHO ARE YOU?

An intelligence who has
always existed ....Abraham 3:22
A child of God ....Hebrews 12:9
Acts 17:29-30

2 WHERE DID YOU
COME FROM?

A pre-existence ....Jeremiah 1:4-5
Where all things were created
spiritually ....Moses 3:5
And where we lived with
God ....D&C 93:21-23, 29

3 WHAT IS CHRIST'S
ORIGIN AND YOUR
RELATIONSHIP
TO HIM?

The same
pre-existence ....John 17:4-5, 8:56-58
Where He was our Elder
Brother ....D&C 93:21-23
And where He was chosen to be
the Creator and the Savior ....Moses 4:1-2
D&C 38:1-4
Abraham 3:24-28
And from whence He became
Jehovah, the God of the
Old Testament ....1 Nephi 19:10
Genesis 1:26

4 WHY ARE YOU
HERE?

To advance as God has
advanced ....TPJS[1] p. 354
To prove yourself ....Abraham 3:24-26
To gain a body ....TPJS, p. 181, 352
D&C 93:34
To gain immortality and
eternal life ....Moses 1:39

5 WHAT ARE THE
OBJECTIVES OF
THIS LIFE?

To have joy ....2 Nephi 2:25
To learn to know God ....John 17:3
To perfect ourselves ....Matthew 5:48
To prepare to meet God ....Alma 34:32

6 WHERE ARE YOU
GOING?

First to the
spirit world ....1 Peter 3:18-19; 4:6
Then, if worthy, back to the
presence of God ....TPJS, p. 310
D&C 76:50-70

7 WHAT WILL YOU
BE LIKE IF YOU
DO RETURN?

Like God and Christ ....1 John 3:2

---

[1]Joseph Fielding Smith (comp.), *Teachings of the Prophet Joseph Smith* (Salt Lake City: Deseret Book Company, 1938).

With Self 23

In retrospect,
the whole question of
"why"
has a known answer.
We need not design it, or work it out, or invent it . . . .
we must merely *learn* it;
and *accept* it;
and *understand* it;
and *fulfill* it.

Chapter 2

Who Are You?

- Who are you?

  See how many answers you can give to that one question.

  List them, as an exercise . . . . as preparation for what follows.

  One person gave forty-eight correct answers in about two minutes. He said:

  An eternal being, a child of God, a brother of Christ
  and of all mankind, a steward over all God has given me,
       a husband,
  a father, a child of earthly parents, a brother of earthly siblings,
  a student, an accountant, a descendant, a Sunday School teacher,
  a Republican, a homeowner, a cousin, a grandson, an elder,
       a temple
  recommend holder, a football fan, an amateur artist, a
       college graduate,
  a careful driver, a friend, an advisor, a basement remodeler,
       a stamp
  collector, a provider, a commuter, a fisherman, a teetotaler,
       a tennis
  player, a Mormon, a home teacher, a six-foot,
  170-pound individual, a Jaycee, a person with an above-
       average IQ, an
  Ephraimite, an American, a mixture of Dutch, Norwegian
       and English,
  a brownette, a resident of Arlington, Virginia, a bird watcher,
  a member of the Second Ward, a reader, a potential millionaire,
  a part-time real estate salesman, an investor.

We asked him to pick the ten most important.
It was relatively easy; he chose:
A child of God,
A brother of Christ,
A steward over all God has given me,
A father,
A child of my parents,
A brother to my brothers and sisters,
A descendant,
A friend,
An elder in the Church,
A husband . . . .
He noticed,
and so did we,
that his choices were all *relationships*.

We asked him to pick the ten at which he spent the most time,
and the most mental energy.
It was easy,
but not pleasant. He had to choose:
An accountant,
A student,
A basement remodeler,
An investor,
A Jaycee,
A commuter,
A stamp collector,
A fisherman,
A part-time real estate salesman,
A football fan (and he had to put this one because he added
　　up the
football hours from the week and the total was greater than
　　those he had spent
with his children).

He noticed,
and so did we,
that this list was primarily oriented to *things*
rather than people.

We went back then,
to his "ten most important" list.
Since they were all relationships, they were all answers
        to the question
"Who are you to ....?"
For example, "a husband" was the answer to the question
"Who are you to your wife?"
We asked him to expand on each of his answers.
He expanded "a husband" into:
"A partner, a helpmeet, a lover, a provider, an encourager, an
appreciator, an advisor, a co-planner, a co-goal-setter, a protector,
a co-child-raiser, a sweetheart, an escort."
We asked the obvious question . . . . "If you are really all of
        those things
to her . . . .
doesn't it consume a great deal of time and mental effort?"
He gave the obvious answer . . . . "I guess it should be on
the other list . . . the list of where I spend the most time and
        mental energy."

Next,
he expanded "a child of God" into:
"A servant, a prayerful man, a debtor who owes all, one of so very
few who has access to the fulness of His Gospel, a holder of His
power, a covenant child, a potentially similar being,
        a representative
with a foreordained mission to fulfill, a disappointment in that I'm

not meeting my full potential, a choice enough spirit child to
be put here in the last days."
He went on until
he had expanded all of his "ten most important" answers,
and he found
that none of them could be fulfilled without considerable time
and mental effort
(not to mention prayer and guidance).

He had originally listed forty-eight things.
He *was* forty-eight things . . . .
And when he expanded each of those, as he had done with the
"ten most important,"
he was literally hundreds of things . . . . and there were hundreds
of answers
to the question "who are you?"
We thought about his answers for a while,
and decided
that, as true as they all were, he really needed only the first four
(the very first four that he initially gave),
for they explained who he actually and eternally was,
and they were inclusive of everything else that he listed
or that he could have listed.

1. An eternal being who has always and will always exist.
2. A spirit child of God.
3. A brother of Christ and of all God's other spirit children.
4. A steward over all that God has given.

Think about that . . . .
You are an eternal being, a child of God, a brother of all . . . .
those have been discussed in the previous chapter,
and they are facts.
What are you beyond these things?
Just one thing . . . .
a *steward*.

● You are a steward over your talents and skills and gifts
          and interests.
   God has given them to you,
   and the use you make of them
   will determine
   your ability to retain them and their ability to grow.
   The scriptures tell us that each person is given a gift.
   The new behaviorists and sociologists now tell us of the
          six categories
   of gifts (and say that everyone is exceptional in at least one):
   Scholastic or academic,
   Communication,
   Planning and goal-striving,
   Decision-making,
   Creative,
   Mechanical and conceptual.
   The listers lack the spiritual insight to mention the
          greater gifts
   of empathy and charity, of openness to the Spirit,
   of sure-knowledge testimony.
   One who struggles and finally discovers his gifts is like a man
   who has been swimming against the current
   and suddenly discovers that it is easier to go downstream . . . .
   and it is certain that one who finds and focuses on his gift
   will make great contributions.

   You are or will become a steward over your own family
          and children.
   You and your spouse will either be exalted together
   or not at all;
   and so your partnership must become a two-way stewardship . . . .
   each responsible for the other.

Such a concept can create a beautiful *contest*
of who can *give* the most.
God's greatest trust is exhibited when he puts a spirit brother
     or sister
(perhaps more noble and great than we)
into our care
to raise, to nurture, to teach, to motivate.
And our valiance in this great stewardship
will determine
their exaltation
as well as our own.

You are a steward over your own physical body.
God has given it to you that you might expand
       your awareness . . . .
Its cleanliness and general state of repair
will determine not only how well it functions here,
but also how it functions
(and what functions it performs)
in its perfected, resurrected state.

You are a steward over your ancestor's destiny
(and your neighbor's destiny)
in the sense
that those who have departed
and have accepted the Gospel on the other side may well be
waiting,
and depending on you for the blessings of the ordinances . . . .
and your neighbor may have no one else to tell him
what he needs to know.

Again, in both cases, their exaltation
and yours
is at stake.

You are a steward over your appetites and passions.
God has given them to you,
and your use of them, your ability to bridle them
(which means to control and channel their power),
will determine whether they lift you to soaring heights
or plummet you to spiritual death.

You are a steward over all of your worldly possessions.
God has given them to you
(no matter how hard you think you have worked for them).
And if their gain is your first priority,
or if their use is inward and self-serving,
you will receive no eternal reward
to replace
the riches that you will lose when you die . . . .
But if they come to you as a by-product, while you pursue
higher priorities,
then it will be clear to you that God has given them to you,
and their use will be outward and selfless.

You are a steward over your opportunities and potentials.
God has given them to you,
and it is within your power to either seize them and fulfill them
or bypass them, fritter them away, allow them to dissolve
through lack of use.

You have stewardship also over the challenges, the difficulties,
the pain
of your life;
and just as a muscle only strengthens through stress
so a great part of us only grows as we experience and overcome
life's vicissitudes.
It is here that some lose faith and say,
"If God made all, then he made pain and sin and violence
and inequality . . . .
therefore, he is not my God."
They err on two levels.
First, in assuming that God made all from nothing
(when in fact He worked within existing laws
and organized existing matter).[1]
Second, in assuming that pain and difficulty are causes and
        not blessings.
Consider the aborigine who returns from a hunt to find a team of
surgeons performing an appendectomy on his more educated
        wife. He makes
three incorrect assumptions: 1. They are trying to hurt or
        kill her.
2. It is happening against her will. 3. The end result will
        not be in
her best interest.
If you think about it carefully, you will find that many
make the same three incorrect assumptions regarding
the tribulations of this life.

You are a steward over your freedom, over your citizenship,
over your country and all its beauties.

---

[1]Doctrine and Covenants 93:29. *Teachings of the Prophet Joseph Smith,*
        pp. 350-352.

God gave us these, and if you live in America
he called your land a land choice above all others,
told us that he raised up and inspired the founding fathers
        of the U.S.A.
and warned us that America would remain choice only on
        conditions of righteousness.
Whether we live in America or in some other free land
it is clear that our stewardship determines
whether we preserve our liberty,
whether we preserve our freedom,
whether we preserve our environment . . . .
and a passive "let others worry" type of stewardship here
(just as anywhere else)
produces failing and disastrous results.

Many of you are stewards over the teachings and doctrines
of the true and complete Gospel of Jesus Christ.
God has given this to only about one in one thousand living,
and if you are in that select number . . . .
Oh how great is your stewardship over attainment
        and distribution . . . .
over learning it well,
and over teaching it well
to the other nine hundred and ninety-nine!

Many are stewards too, over the very power of God . . . .
over His Priesthood,
and there is
simply
no greater stewardship
than that.

We are all stewards over our callings and responsibilities
and foreordinations . . . .
For every person comes to this life with specific missions to fulfill,
and the rewards for finding and fulfilling come in the form of
expanded eternal potential.

It is true then . . . .
we are eternal spirit children of God and siblings of Christ
and beyond that, during this earthly sojourn,
we are *stewards*.

So the question of "who,"
like the question of "why,"
has a *known* answer,
and together they provide a solid foundation for your relationship
with yourself
and a launching pad from which to confront
two questions of basic self-evaluation,
which are . . . .
"where"
and
"how."

Chapter 3

Where Are You?

• I sat one day above a beaver pond
in a high mountain forest.
I had a basic idea of my location . . . . could have guessed my
latitude and longitude . . . . knew how to walk back out of the hills.
Yet my mind's private conversation that day
was on the question of where I was.
I looked into the pond's reflection and could see down,
into the sky,
forever.
If time goes forever forward and forever back
and if space never ends in any direction . . . .
then how can one ever measure where he is . . . . since there are
no known compass points, no grid coordinates?
Just how do we locate ourselves, and
how can we ever really know
where we are?

● Then,
    gradually,
    I realized that we do have some known locations
    from which to orient our position . . . .
    We have the compass point of God's objective for us
    (which is perfection)
    and we can locate where we are in relation to that point . . . .
    We also have the grid coordinates of eternal progression
    (and of the role which we know this earth life must play
    in that progression)
    and we can locate our position in relation to those coordinates . . . .
    Finally, we have the roadmap of our patriarchal blessings
    (which give us insights into our callings,
    our missions,
    our foreordinations)
    and we can locate where we are on that map
    in relation to where we are supposed to be.

    On a map, we measure by plotting the ground we
    have covered
    against that which is left to travel
    and,
    having never traveled that way before, we need a good map to
    make the measurement.
    So are our lives . . . .
    Scriptures and the Gospel's teachings give us a general outline map,
    and provide some compass points and coordinates,
    but still leave much to guesswork . . . .

A patriarchal blessing, on the other hand,
is personal, individually tailored scripture
which can fill in the contour lines
and draw the specific roads and interchanges
that we should follow . . . .
thus permitting meaningful measurement
of where we are.

If your road map was done in topographical relief,
you would see that it is not level . . . .
no one's is . . . .
because there is always a gap between where you are and
where you should be . . . .
and the gap is filled with boulders and crevices
and perhaps some quicksand.
To get across the gap,
two coordinates must be known correctly and absolutely . . . .
One is "exactly where you are"
and the other is "exactly where you want to be."
The only way to find the first one
is by locating the second one.
(Because we can only know where we are
in relation
to where we want to be.)

As valuable as the patriarchal blessing road map is,
it is not easy to read . . . .
and one who tries to decipher it by himself

may inject some personal interpretation
and end up climbing the wrong mountain.
So remember that you need personal inspiration
through communicating prayer
to fully understand your blessing.
(The blessing itself is proof that God knows you
far better
than you know yourself . . . .
so naturally you need His inspiration to read
between its lines
and to comprehend all that it really says.)

No two patriarchal blessings are alike,
because each person has a different destination and because each person
is unique . . . .
That uniqueness, that individuality that you were born with,
is not only something to appreciate and to recognize . . . .
it is something to protect . . . .
to fight for in a world that seems to thrive on
convention
and sameness.
Of all lessons, the lesson of uniqueness is simultaneously
the most valuable
and the most difficult to learn.
Yet, if you can once catch the vision that God,
your Heavenly Father,
knows what you actually are, and that he loves the *real* you

(which is something that no one else is) . . . .
then you will be proud of the good there is in you,
and secure in all you can become.

The key lies in learning to act rather than react,
and in stepping to the beat of the drummer you hear.
(Which is made difficult by the
stereotyped symphony
of what is accepted by society,
and the blaring broadcast of other people's aspirations
for you.)

Take your blessing (or get one if you haven't one)
and make a serious evaluation.
Look at the promises and indications in the blessing . . . .
list them . . . .
use them as a map . . . .
plot how far you've gone toward each.
Analyze the gap between where you are and where you
        ought to be.
With your blessing, the scriptures,
and all the self-knowledge you have gained,
as guides,
sit down and try to write "where you should be"
in less than fifty words.
(It will be harder to do it in fifty than in five-hundred.)
Then do the same thing with "where you actually are."
Survey the distance between the two.

Formulate plans to bridge the difference,
and plot a reasonable course leading from one to the other.
Finally, have the tenacity and follow-through to stay
on that course . . . .
to avoid the diversions and distractions
that lead nowhere.

The "why" and "who" questions did not require you to evaluate . . .
they didn't have to,
because their answers are known and set.
But the "where" question is different
because the answer is not given, and
because your answer will be different from everyone else's.

Chapter 4

How Are You?

- Since you are plural,
  the title question is plural.
  How are you physically?
  emotionally?
  socially?
  mentally?
  spiritually?
  Why ask the questions?
  Because you can't have a full-blown relationship
  with anyone
  (including yourself)
  until you know those answers . . . .
  and you can't help the person you're relating to
  to improve
  (even if that person is yourself)
  until you know where the improvement is needed.

• How are you physically?
Reflect again on the fact that you are a steward over
your body . . . .
and that its condition and running order
can't help but influence the spirit and mind and emotions
inside it
any more than the condition of a refrigerator
can help influencing the preservation of its contents.
Do you recall that you and the other hosts
of the earlier world
shouted for joy
at the notion of inheriting flesh and bones . . . .
not for the pain and limitation we knew they would include
but for the joy . . . . the joy
of smelling honeysuckle,
of tasting a just-picked strawberry,
of hearing the unsilence of a "silent" forest,
of watching the sun's colors caught in one bead of water
just set to drop from the leaf,
of feeling the texture of a loved one's hair . . . .
You say that all possess these five senses?
On the contrary . . . .
Most possess dulled mutations of these gifts . . . .
dimmed by lack of use, by lack of appreciation, and by years of
existence in a mistreated, poorly maintained body.
Most never achieve the natural "high" that comes through
sensing all five senses
simultaneously.

To be seeing
and aware of what you're seeing,
hearing and aware of what you're hearing,
feeling and aware of what you're feeling,
smelling and aware of what you're smelling,
tasting and aware of what you're tasting,
all at once,
is a sensational experience
even if you're just walking down the street.

Most of us know the joy of using a well-maintained tool.
It feels right,
It works well,
It gives satisfaction.
Like so many things . . . . we know
the validity of the principle
but neglect its most important application.

● How are you mentally?
Another reason for the pre-existent shouts of joy
was the anticipated learning opportunity . . . .
An earth laboratory which we knew
would facilitate a certain type of learning
for a short span of years.
Yet now, *within* that short span,
we are told (by specialists) that we use only 10 percent
of the capacity
of our minds.

Again, there is a vivid connection to the other four "yous"
because
unfit bodies,
stagnant emotions,
dormant spirits
result, at least in part, from unstimulated minds which,
in turn,
result from the nonthinking acceptance of
other people's ideas,
other people's methods,
other people's styles and values.
By accepting these, we forfeit the great joy of thinking freely
and put to sleep whatever creative evaluation powers
we may have.

Instead . . . .
learn to design your own destiny.

Instead . . . .
love yourself (as God does) for what you really are . . . . and
accept the Lord's words and methods and values . . . .
for they will expand your intellect rather than shrink it
and lift you
to the level of their Author.

Instead . . . .
seek communication with great minds . . . . take the risk
of feeling inferior
as you talk to one whose mind can awaken yours.
(If it is true that a muscle strengthens when stretched,
then it is even more true
of the mind.)

Instead . . . .
break your routine, get out of a numbing pattern . . . .
begin to act rather than react . . . .
and learn the joy of a free mind.

● How are you emotionally?
  How do you feel?
  Emotions, you know, are not passive, inconsequential notions
  that hide inside.
  Emotions determine who we are . . . . and what we do.
  Consider
  the contagious power of happiness;
  the inner-kindled strength that somehow accompanies
  our greatest sorrow;
  the real joy of feeling (anything) deeply.

  There is so much talk about containing and subduing the emotions.
  Isn't it really more a question
  of understanding them
  and of bridling them (or harnessing their power)?
  "Moods" are generally thought of negatively . . . .
  (to be moody is bad).
  But try to think of a mood that is not potentially productive.

  Remorse, in its productive sense,
  generates repentance.
  Anger, in its productive sense,
  is called righteous indignation.
  Depression, in its productive sense,
  brings serious pondering and needed resolution.
  Rainy days make things grow.

  So all moods may be productive . . . .
  but going beyond that, there are two particularly effective

moods, two "mental patterns" which generate the highest form
of human achievement and produce the most dramatic results.
One is a "*lightning*" mood.
In it, you are happy and confident and active and charismatic
and achieving . . . .
and a lot gets *done*.
The other is a "*waves*" mood.
In it, you are calm and restful and wound-down and thoughtful
and creative . . . .
and a lot gets *thought*.

The lightning fills up your achievement needs and
makes you capable of feeling the waves.
The waves create the blueprints
for the next lightning to build from.
One feeds the other, and one feeds *on* the other
and if neither is there
the other has a harder time coming.

At any given moment, you are relatively close to one of the two.
In a mood that we usually think of as a negative
"letdown"
we may be very close to the "waves,"
and in a mood that we usually think of as a negative
hyper-active frustration
we may be very close to "lightning."
Learn the art of bumping yourself from a negative mood
into its productive counterpart,

and learn
to promote the self-perpetuating "wave-lightning" alternation.

Emotions are real things
which possess qualities and properties that can be
analyzed and measured
and changed.
Experiments at leading universities have discovered
a human "aura" .... a *glow*
which radiates from all of us, which changes when our
        moods change,
and which affect the auras of others around us.

● How are you socially?
   Do you look into mirrors . . . . or through windows?
   Do you see situations mirrored
   to reflect their impact on your own turned-in life . . . .
   or can you see through windows and sensitize yourself
   to the needs and motivations and feelings
   of others?
   The question is applicable to everything from
   how you drive your car
   to how you formulate the objectives of your life.

   From that view, there is another way
   to think of
   the golden rule . . . .
   "As you would have others do unto you" is an expression
   of loving intent rather than of specific action.
   Are others the same as you
   (in their perspectives, their objectives, their requirements
   for happiness)?
   The fact is that they are *not* just like you . . . .
   no one is.
   So,
   "Do unto others as they would want you to do unto them,"
   always provided that their wants are legitimate.
   (And look through the window enough to know
   what those wants are.)

   We talk of "social skills" as though *they* were numerous and
   diverse and complex.
   Actually,
   the major portion of this "they" is an "it" called

"listening" . . . .
listening in its broadest definition so that it really means
"receiving inputs and feedbacks through all seasons."
Listen to what people feel as well as what they say.
Listen to know what encouragement, what compliment, what praise
will make their day.
Listen enough to know what questions to ask so that you can
listen some more.

There is a reverse side to the listening coin . . . .
one that we usually forget.
When you are listening you are *giving* your ear, your attention,
your concern,
possibly your advice.
Real relationships require a capacity to receive
as well as to give.
You can receive another's concern and help
only if you can be open enough to share with him your honest
feelings . . . .
your inner self and its realities.
Think back on how the barriers dropped the last time someone
opened to you
his personal problem . . . .
and think how you tried to help . . . . and later
shared one of your own with him.
If one pitcher pours its contents into another,
we have one that's too full and one that's too empty
and no mixing of the mix.

There is a great joy in windows,
in listening,
in giving and receiving.
Christ was the most acutely aware of these joys . . . .
They are an important part of the quality
He called "charity."

• How are you spiritually?
. . . . quite a question,
because
on its answer may hang your ultimate ability to enter
the celestial kingdom.
Peter spoke of the celestial prerequisites . . . . [1]
(actually, he called them requirements "to make your calling and
election sure" . . . . but that calling and election is a
promise
of celestial glory,
so one's requirements are the other's.)
Peter listed eight:
Faith, virtue, knowledge, temperance, patience, godliness,
brotherly kindness, charity.
These aren't eight separate, distinguishable qualities . . . .
they are eight ways of saying one quality . . . .
eight ways of saying:
"Be Christ-like."

Most of us have a mental picture
of what it means to be Christ-like . . . .
Today's words are "sensitivity," "extra-centeredness," "congruency,"
"warmth," "concern."
But whatever the adjectives, we *feel*
what "Christ-like" means.
To test yourself is frightening . . . .
Are you Christ-like when you drive?

---

[1] 2 Peter 1:5-10.

when you pass by the beggar?
when your ambition steps on and over others?
when you react to someone who has offended you?
when you choose your own goal over an opportunity to
    help another?

How are you spiritually . . . .
(And, of course, the question is really one of Relationships
with God . . . . but shift to it for a moment now . . . .)
How accessible are you to the Holy Ghost,
and how much do you exercise your right
to His constant companionship?
Our forefathers faced the temptation of hardship and persecution.
Most of us face the temptation of acceptance and relative
    well-being.
Many of them dropped out because it was too hard.
Many of us drop out because it's too easy.
Ours is the challenge of developing humility and spirituality
that is not crisis-induced.
Most of us have felt our greatest dependency
and prayed our greatest prayers
in the face
of some real problem . . . . some major crisis over which
we felt no control and in which we needed
great help.
The humility which results from the dependency,
when converted into prayer and supplication,
can bring about an in-pouring of beyond-the-self strength
from God.

The problem is that the strength is then *used* to combat
and overcome the crisis
which induced it . . . .
and it is dissipated in that effort.
Imagine for a moment the good that could be achieved
with a measure of that same strength generated not by
crisis-response humility,
but by *success-accompanied humility*
(which must be the rarest of commodities).

• After you've decided how you think you are,
  You ought to see if others agree . . . .
  because if others don't see you as you really are,
  (or if they do . . . . and you don't)
  then both *being* and *changing* lose their motivation.
  It's a question of how "congruent" you are . . . (in other words,
  how closely your self-image matches the image you project
         to others).

  Look at Auragām (page 57)
  It's a game you can play . . . .
  a device for plotting self-image against projected image.
  First rank yourself from one to five on each quality by marking
  the dots on a transparent sheet (acetate, tissue, or whatever)
  laid over the page
  (the fifth dot out is best, the first is worst, three is average).
  Then connect the dots you've made to form an "aura" . . . . or an
  outline around the figure.
  Now remove the clear sheet you have marked
  and have *someone else* rank you
  on another transparent sheet.
  Then overlay the two sheets on the illustration and evaluate
         the close parts and the spreads.

  The real learning will come not in playing the game,
  but in *discussing* it . . . . from asking and answering the questions
  that the game promotes . . . .
  Was he honest or tactful in his rankings . . . . which were you?
  What led him to mark you as a "4" on "spontaneous" while
  you marked yourself as a "1"?

Which traits are most important . . . . which are irrelevant?
Etc.
Etc.

There are many variations of the game . . . .
such as plotting the evaluation of an old friend against that of
a new acquaintance.
Each variation should be designed to help you see yourself
as others see you.

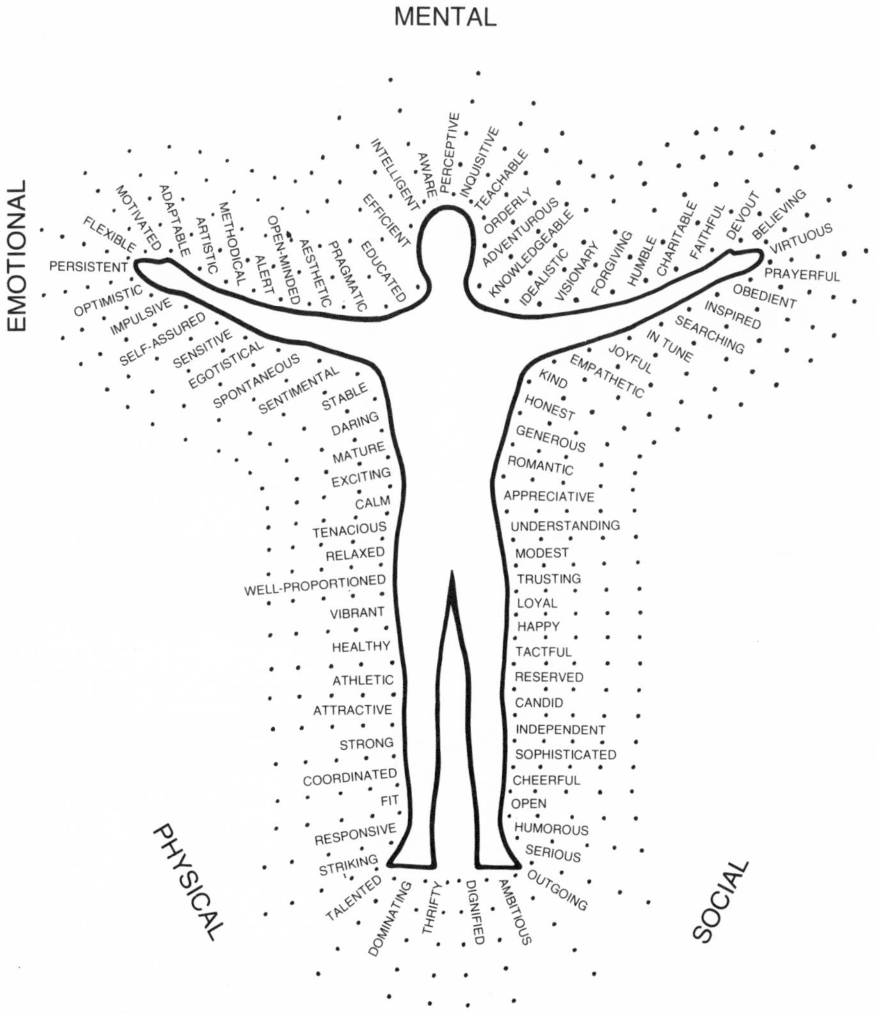

The Auragām concept was created by Richard Rosine.

● In retrospect,
  this is a chapter on "joys."
  And the question "How are you?" can be rephrased to read,
  "How many of the joys do you feel?"
  The joy of feeling deeply . . . .
  The joy of a well-maintained tool . . . .
  The joy of simple things . . . .
  The joy of thinking freely . . . .
  The joy of giving and receiving and of being needed . . . .
  The joy of non-crisis-induced humility . . . .
  The joy of congruency.
  How many? How often?

  We have now asked two questions (who, why) and *given*
  their answers . . . .
  We have asked two more questions (where, how) and asked *you*
  to give your own honest, evaluative answers . . . .
  We now want to ask two last questions (what, when) and have you
  decide
  what their answers will be
  in your case.

Chapter 5

What Are You?

- Have you ever pondered how
  incredibly fortunate you are *not to know* the answer
  to the question leading this chapter?
  We do not know . . . . it has not been given or predestined.
  Rather,
  we determine it.
  The blessing of not knowing, and of thus being able to determine
  "what we are,"
  is called free agency . . . .
  and each of us voted for it . . . . and it won out in a
  pre-existent election
  over a proposal wherein "what we are" would have been
  decided and dictated
  by one who was then called "a son of the morning."[1]

  Do not misunderstand . . . . we *do* know
  who we are and why we are . . . through revelations from God;
  and there is an attempt to summarize those answers
  in earlier chapters.
  But *what* you are and *what* you will become
  is yours to decide,
  and that agency will be the root of your eternal reward
  or your eternal regret.

---

[1]Doctrine and Covenants 76:26.

In the "who" and "why" chapters you were only called on for
attention, and comprehension, and retention.
In the "where" and "how" chapters
you had to carefully analyze, realistically evaluate.
But now . . . .
with the first four answers in your head,
you must prioritize,
and decide,
and resolve,
and plan,
and implement,
and become . . . .
Only if you do this can you make "what you are"
a question of *design* rather than one
of chance.

In the ultimate, knowing what to strive for
is simple.
God told us to "be perfect" . . . . and the earth has had only
one illustration of perfection.
Therefore, "what" should ultimately be "Christ-like."

Another way to state that basic
is within the notion of striving for celestial glory . . . .
and we know so very clearly that those who go there
"will be like Him."[1]
So again the analysis output answer to the ultimate "what"
is "Christ-like."

---

[1] 1 John 3:2.

● But now, ask the question of
how to get between the present "what"
and the ultimate "what" . . . .
Which sequence of "beings" and "becomings"
will ferry you across . . . . from one to the other?
And what is the "what" for right now and for the
"seeable"
four- or five-year future?
In other words, What . . . . now?
What will you be . . . . ?
and What will you do . . . . ?
(And the questions *need* to be answered,
whether you're 17 or 71.)

Even among those who possess the Gospel's answers . . . .
(even among those who realize that they are one in a thousand
possessing restored truths and who, therefore, conclude
that their "what" must somehow be connected
with the implementation or distribution of those truths . . . .)
even among these, there are a number of different
schools of thought:

"Number one" reasons that great contributions can only be made
through and with the influence and the freedom
of relative wealth,
so *his* immediate "what" is the stockpiling of lucre
which he sees
as the means to full-time, influential, *future*
service to God and to the building of His kingdom.

"Number two" says,
"Why wait to build when that kingdom needs
so many carpenters
right now?"
Why not work for the Church . . . . a teacher, an administrator . . . .
a public relations expert . . . .
Whatever you do
or think you can do,
chances are that the Church needs it . . . .
so why not let that need serve as the answer to your "what" . . . .
and why not make your contribution your vocation
rather than your avocation?

"Number three" sees the danger that "number one" may
    still be saying
"I'll give it all up and contribute when I get just a little more"
when he's sixty-five years old . . . .
Yet, unlike "number two," number three decides
he does not want to mix his Kingdom-building activities
with his livelihood . . . .
so he says that his immediate "what" is an occupation which
requires a minimum amount of his time and creative energy
so that he can save both
for Church and family.

"Number four" disagrees in the sense that he believes
that creative energy
(like love and certain other good things)
is not something you use up . . . .

but rather
something that multiplies and grows as you use it.
So his occupational "what" is something challenging
into which he tries to graft
good example
and missionary-oriented invitations to Church,
and a Christ-like character.

• All four of these "whats"
contain some good seeds . . . . some right direction . . . . some
valid fact;
but each, in its own way, is myopic . . . . and each,
even in its purest and most ideal form,
is applicable only to a certain limited number of people.
So, rather than *recommend* any specific approach or any specific
hybrid composite of approaches
(which would violate the earlier premise that
only you
can determine your "what"),
let us instead list some true principles
which you should have in mind in discovering and approaching
your *own* immediate "what."

1. Happiness and "having a worthy cause"
walk with linked arms.
You'd think that, if you had something worth more to you
than anything else,
that thing would be worth a great deal . . . .
yet,
if you have nothing in life worth more than life itself,
then life itself is not worth very much to you . . . .
and that may be the key to what a wise man meant when he
spoke of the joy of risking life,
and of having a cause.

2. The Lord *wants* you to know His will for your "what."
(He almost pleads for you to ask . . . . "Ask and ye
shall receive . . . . Knock and it shall be opened . . . .)[1]

3. Whatever your "what" is, your family *is*
first priority.
("The greatest work that you'll ever do is within the walls
of your own home.")[2]
And the next highest priority
belongs to the Church.
(Anyone with certain mental and physical abilities can make
a contribution involving *worldly* skills and knowledge
and can thus hack away at the leaves on the tree of human
problems. But only a few . . . . those with the Gospel's
insight . . . . have the potential of chopping through the roots.)

4. You live
in the greatest and most fascinating era
of this earth's history.
(Today's world is like the Mayflower . . . . the horizon is
so broad and so unknown, but more
reachable
than ever before. How important it is, therefore, to be
a part of your age.)

5. Fulfillment comes in direct proportion to the
"long-lastingness"
of that with which we work.

---

[1] Doctrine and Covenants 4:7.
[2] President Harold B. Lee.

Some things are *un*-lasting
(most "deals," most "memorandums," most "routine assignments")
and to work with them is *unfulfilling*.
Some things last *relatively* long
(A house, a contract, a worthwhile project)
and to work with them is *relatively* fulfilling.
Some things last for *eternity*
(Families, this earth, people, relationships, animals)
and to work with them is *eternally* fulfilling.

6. The inclination to
create
is spiritually inherited, and the difference between
those who create and those who do not
is staggering.

7. One of the two things that is predictable about
the future
is that we can't predict it . . . .
the other is that it will not be the same as now.
If you can design your "what" on the basis of the future,
it will fit better when you get there.

8. A good approach for discovering your immediate "what"
is to start by listing your strengths.
All have gifts . . . . and you *know*, somewhere in you,
what yours are.
List what you like to do, and what you do well
(it's the same list)

and then open your mind
to everything . . . .
get outside the limiting ideas of where you grew up
and the limiting parameters of what others around you
have done . . . . then,
when you are sure that you are acting and not reacting,
list *everything*
that your abilities could potentially allow you to do.
Then, choose from among them (by the Lord's decision-making
process . . . . study, pray, analyze, decide tentatively,
get God's confirmation of the correctness of your decision).
If you are twenty-one this whole process may be termed
        "evaluation" . . . .
(getting on the right track).
If you are forty-eight this whole process may be termed
        "re-evaluation" . . . .
(being sure you *are* on the right track).
The two are equally important.

Then, bring all the strengths you have listed to bear
on achieving the things
you have chosen.

9. "Whats" become far more useful when they are refined
into specific objectives
and confined into a timetable not longer than five years.
They can then be broken down from there
into workable, year-long chunks.

If you can put these true principles into a bag
along with your own personal desires and inclinations
and shake them up just right,
perhaps you can dump out your own "whats"
and stack them up in front of you.

● When you look at your "whats"
you ought to find two basic types . . . . *achievement goals*
and *relationship goals*.

An achievement goal is acceptance at a certain graduate school,
or publishing a certain book
or saving a certain sum
or obtaining a certain position.
They are measurable, they are specific (the more specific
the better), and they can be
chopped up
into sub-objectives.
These are *achievement* goals . . . . *they are important*.

A relationship goal is to be a better father,
or to tell your friends about the Gospel,
or to draw closer to God,
or to better understand yourself . . . .
They can be measured only relatively,
they are sometimes hard to state specifically and,
while you may be able to define and break out their components,
you probably cannot set up any particular sequence of *stages*
by which they are obtained.
These are *relationship* goals . . . . *they are essential*.

The seeking process for achievement goals is different
        from that for
relationship goals.
Achievement goals require:

1. sub-division (so that a staircase of specific minors leads
to a specific major), and
2. tenacity, (so that you stay on that staircase no matter
what tries to blow you off), and
3. a bit of serendipity (which simply means that you are
not so involved in looking down at the steps
that you miss the chance to leap-frog over some
or even to grab the banister and swing yourself up onto
a higher staircase).
A good achievement goal is (at the same time)
idealistic, realistic, and pragmatic.

Relationship goals, on the other hand, call for a process
of programming the subconscious . . . .
of being so *aware* of the goal, and *wanting* it so badly,
that it happens . . . .
(No one develops a real relationship because of some
stainless-steel plan for relating . . . .
he develops it because he wants it.)

The two kinds of goals do not work at cross purposes with
      each other.
In fact,
they go together and need each other to survive.
One who achieved countless *things*
but formed no relationships would be an object of
pity
(and the whole notion fails anyway . . . .
because real achievement *involves* relationships).

One who relates well but is void of achievement
is a fictitious being.
He *could not* relate well
because he would have nothing to contribute to a
relationship
and few if any would wish to relate to him.

It is hard to pursue both types of goals
at the same instant,
just as it is hard to have "waves" and
"lightning" mental patterns together.
But you can be totally *conscious* of both
and seek them alternately
and as complements to each other.

(Incidentally, "waves" facilitate the pursuit and
successful achievement of sensitive
relationship goals . . . . "lightning" works to
the credit of strong achievement goals.)

Now,
If you have *designed* your own personal "whats,"
go on
to the last question in this section
the question of "when."

Chapter 6

When Are You?

● After all the other questions are answered . . . .
   after you've *discovered* who you are and why you are,
   after you've *determined* where you are and how you are
   after you've *decided* what you are and what you wish to be
   it comes down to the question
   of "when,"
   and the wrong answer to that question
   makes the right answers to the other five
   useless
   Life offers us two precious gifts:
   one is the free agency spoken of in the previous chapter
   the other is time . . . . and time is the substance
   from which to formulate the answer to this chapter's question
   of "when."
   The two gifts work together, for it is free agency that
   allows us
   to exchange our allotment of earthly time
   for whatever we wish.

   So turn your thoughts to the topic of time . . . .
   time, which must someday be accounted for;
   time,
   which exists in unlimited supply in eternity and which
   exists in limited supply in this finite segment of infinite eternity.

This earth laboratory
contains the apparatus and opportunity necessary
to perform innumerable experiments,
and the formulas on the scripture-blackboard give guidance
regarding the question of *which* procedures and activities are
most beneficial and most fulfilling and most eternally important.
The thing to remember is
that we are allowed only one period
in the laboratory . . . .
then we move on . . . .
with or without the
knowledge and experience and progress
that the laboratory offered us.

As the infinite amount of time contained in eternity
is segmented,
so should we segment the finite amount of time that
we have here . . . .
for to everything there is a season
and the shortness of our lives makes wasted time
a sin of omission,
and misspent time a sin of commission.

Is that too great a simplification? . . . . to say that
there are only three kinds of time . . . .
well-used time
misused time
and unused time . . . .

one productive, one counterproductive, one unproductive?
Think through the definitions before you answer . . . .

Well-used time is time spent in the pursuit of
correctly derived
relationship goals and achievement goals.
(And this might include everything from taking time
to smell and feel a flower . . . .
which is unmistakably the pursuit of a relationship goal . . . .
to putting in a hard day at a job which you see as worth while . . . .
which is an achievement goal.)
Well-used time is either lightning or waves . . . . or
efforts to "get into"
one or the other.

Misused time is time spent in the pursuit of
wrong or hurtful goals.

Unused time is time spent in the pursuit of
no goals.

● The real "when" question, then, relates back to the
  previous chapter . . . .
  When are you going to achieve your relationship goals?
  When are you going to achieve your achievement goals?
  When and how and in what order?
  (For a goal without a plan [regardless of its elegance
        and correctness]
  is no more than a dream.)

There are some tools
that are helpful in planning the pursuit of both types of goals.
The toolbox follows.
Look through it and see if you find anything you like.
If you do,
please use it free . . . .
and custom-build tools of your own to replace any that
don't quite work for you.

1. Implementation Board:
Once you know what relationships and achievements you
        are willing to
trade your time for,
how about writing them down, so they're finite and physical
and on personal display
to you.
Make a chart of some kind and spell out the achievement goals
on one side
and the relationship goals on the other.
Put it somewhere prominent in your own
private territory

and let it into your mind often enough
that it feels at home there.
Make it the focal point of your *Sunday Sessions* (which is
the next tool in the box).

2. Sunday Sessions:
We talk about what *not* to do on Sunday more than about
what *to* do.
Try thinking of Sundays as a time for making your "when"
        decisions . . . .
for deciding what achievements and what relationships
you will trade your time for.
Doing so will give you a feeling of purpose and direction
throughout the rest of the week.

Take a solid hour or two
and use some sort of timing device to create intensity.
(An hourglass is best.)
Review the goals on the implementation board . . . .

Measure and mark progress on the *achievement* staircase;
think through the connecting links between five-year goals
and their 5:1 ratio one-year goals.
Then move down another mental notch to the
12:1 ratio one-month goals . . . . and finally . . . . *write down*
the *one-week goals* that this whole process will dictate to you.
Review with an open mind . . . .
alter the goals in a perfecting way as you see new opportunities
and as you mature and progress in your perspectives.

Re-program your subconscious *relationship* awareness system.
Evaluate your relationships with God, with self,
with family, with others . . . . .
seek guidance in making plans that will reinforce and deepen
these relationships.

Remember that while Sunday Sessions deal with plans for
    the future,
their *goal* is not to cause you to *live* in the future . . . .
rather, it is to make the *present* (this week)
magnificent.

If you're married, hold part of the Sunday Session jointly.
Feel the power and the bond of setting goals together.
(Don't invite the kids . . . . Family Home Evening comes tomorrow.)
End the joint part of your Sunday Session with testimonies,
born exclusively to each other.

On Fast Sundays, make it a monthly session . . . . bite a
one-month chunk off of the yearly goals so that, weekly you
have to go only to 4:1 rather than 52:1.

3. Progressive Partial Perfection Program:
Benjamin Franklin had a system
that focused attention and effort on particular traits
which he wished to attain and perfect.
His list included things like
Temperance,
Frugality,

Industry,
and his system was to concentrate on *one* for a full week,
with the goal of perfection . . . .
then on another the next week.
Some do the same thing with more closely defined
Gospel principles . . . .
tithing, word of wisdom, observance of the Sabbath,
etc.,
building a list of the things in which they have
developed perfection (or at least total obedience).

Another adaptation uses a similar procedure
to develop desired *personality* traits.
One man wrote out a description of his ideal self . . . .
then picked the key adjectives from it,
and concentrated on *being* one of them each week.
There were eleven words on his particular list,
so he spent at least five weeks on each word each year
and, over time,
became
the ideal self that his words described.

4. Journal:
Whether entries come daily or weekly or "once in a while,"
journals force reflection and re-evaluation
and they clarify and underscore the recurring notions
that are trying from inside
to tell you something.

5. Prayer, Planning, Confidence, Calmness sequence:
Each day is potentially a masterpiece . . . .
and should, therefore, be started by
Prayer (of the two-way, communicating, dialogue type) and
Planning (not by five-minute detail, but by daily objective).
Together, these can bring about a
confidence
and an accompanying calmness
that mellows and beautifies the whole world . . . .
and that magnifies the pure, clear, noble, Camelot qualities
that are inside all of us.
The resulting calm, peaceful clarity of the Holy Ghost's presence
is the most wonderful feeling
known to man.

• The five foregoing "tools" are designed and conceived to aid
    in accomplishing
a particular task . . . .
the task of re-evaluating and implementing achievement
and relationship goals.
That task, during this short mortal probation,
is so vital that it deserves the best designed and
most effective tools possible.
Devise your own . . . .
create them with care,
and use them to hook together
this earth's
goal pieces of your eternal destiny.
You will thus develop a sequence
of answers
to the question
"when?" . . . .
And at least the first part of your answer should be
"now."

• What's wrong with most people's Relationships with themselves?

Well . . . . one or more of the following list:

They don't spend enough time with themselves (alone).
They don't trust themselves.
They don't admit or communicate their own feelings to self.
They're not honest and sincere and open with themselves.
They don't know enough about themselves and their personalities.
They don't respect or admire themselves.
They do not think of themselves as interesting.
They have no commitment to a cause.
They're not gentle and tolerant and patient with themselves.
They don't accept personal challenge or stimulation.
They don't love themselves or take delight in their callings.
They don't understand themselves.
They do not feel the fulfillment of true progression.

Does the list seem familiar?
That is because it is essentially the same as the list
back on pages 6 and 7.
Go back to that list and look at it . . . .
components of an ideal relationship . . . .
Do they all apply to a relationship with self?
There's no question about it . . . . every one does.

It is most important, therefore, for you to know,
that your relationship with yourself can meet the criteria

of every component on that list
if you can accurately and correctly answer the question of
Why and Who and Where and How and What and When
YOU are.

PART II

Relationships ...with Family

"The most important work you will ever do will be within the walls of your own home."

Chapter 7

The First Priority

- I sat one night in seat 8 F and watched the runway lights
  coming up to meet me
  and smiled at the joy I felt welling up
  in anticipation of seeing my family.
  Only three days away, but long enough to focus and fan
  the love and pride and joy.
  It occurred to me that no other landing in any other place could
  arouse feelings to compare.
  The lights below could be the most exotic
  or luxurious
  or adventurous spot on earth . . . .
  could represent any level of fame or fortune . . . .
  could even be the landing lights for the return of a
  space flight hero . . . . with me as hero . . . .
  and still,
  none of these would produce the level of emotion and joy
  that I felt then . . . .
  just going home.

  It was so apparent to me on that night . . . . and always is when
  my thoughts are clear . . . .
  The family is the essence . . . . the family is the joy-source . . . .
  the family is the first priority.

Can you think of any two statements of more absolute
truth and clarity
than President David O. McKay's
"No other success can compensate for failure in the home"
or President Harold B. Lee's
"The most important work you will ever do will be within the walls
of your own home"?
Any man to whom these statements are less than crystal clear
and diamond-hard
and compass-true
is not totally alive, and has no understanding of this earth
or of what came before it
or of what comes after it.
If you lose your family, it matters not at all what else you gain.

If the average man devoted even half as much time
and thought
and creative energy
to his family
as he does to his career . . . .
then the average man would be a far-above-average
      husband and father.

• We're going to assume that readers know a first priority
  when they see one . . . .
  and thus devote this part not to "whys" (which are so apparent)
  but to "hows" (which are often so unapparent).

In keeping with that idea, let us begin by saying that there are
at least four pillars
on which a successful first priority (family) should be built:
1. The *sharing* of the family
2. The *spirit* of the family
3. The *order* of the family
4. The *pride* and *traditions* of the family

The goal here is to extend to you
some ideas
on how to induce all four.
You may want to clutch some of the ideas verbatim,
and use them just as they stand.
Others may chain-react your own "how"-notions
(which is probably even better).

● 1. *Let's begin with sharing.*
Sharing is a transaction in which both the *sharer* and the *sharee* benefit.
The sharee receives the joy and honor of being given to . . . .
and the sharer gains the fulfillment and reward of giving.

But it goes even further than that.
One who shares
sees more,
hears more,
lives more . . . .
because having someone to share sights and sounds and life with magnifies and intensifies
all things.

A sharing family grows individually and collectively
in awareness,
in knowledge,
in unity,
and in charity,
and teaches adults as well as children
to see through the windows of their lives instead of
into its mirrors.

But again, the question is . . . . how?
How about sharing *observations* by having a "family interest book"?
(Not bank interest but mind interest.)

Hang a book of blank paper in a prominent place . . . .
and make an entry when you notice a bird's nest in the old tree,
or how green the grass is where the rain spout comes out,
or the sound a stone makes when it bounces across the
        hollow patio,
or any other sight or sound or smell or taste or feel
that sparks some small smiling in your heart.
Another family member can share your joy when he reads
        your entry,
and it might just be the little "pickup" that
makes his day.
You'll find that you notice more for others
than you ever did for yourself.

How about sharing *appreciation* by having a "family-favorite-
        things wall"
(some big space where you actually write with a marking pen)?
A place where you can share and remember the simple *things*
        in life
that bring you joy . . . .
from fuzzy kittens to the smell of just-mowed hay . . . . and
from Carmel, California, to toasted (but not burned)
        marshmallows . . . .
from your favorite song to your favorite tree . . . .
You'll end up taking less of life for granted,
and you'll like *others* better by knowing
what they like.

How about sharing *discoveries* by having a "family round table"?
When you read a good book or see an interesting article or
find a beautiful picture,
bring it home . . . .
put it on the round table . . . .
let others grow from whatever it is and enjoy it

as you did.
You'll expand your collective horizons,
and it won't be long before
you'll belong to a broadly educated and widely read family.

● 2. *"The spirit of the family"*
might mean the degree of calmness, the degree of peace . . . .
or might mean the presence of the Holy Ghost.
Both are important,
and each encourages the other;
but since the latter inevitably produces the former
(and since the reverse is not necessarily true),
it is the specific Spirit of the Holy Ghost that should be
actively sought.

A home with His Spirit is
an oasis of calm within the high-strung desert of the world;
and the Spirit is the solder that welds family members
together
in a relationship bond of eternal strength.

The Holy Ghost should become the third partner
in the marriage partnership,
because a oneness can be better achieved between the three
than between the two.

Children easily (though subconsciously) feel the Holy Ghost's
presence.
His calming influence of love and charity can produce a
harmony
and an even, steady nature, and an obedience
that is well beyond the limits or capacities of any
earthly expert in child psychology or interpersonal behavior.

It is the presence of His Spirit that can make a home
into what a prophet has called
the very closest approximation of what heaven will be.
His presence teaches children the freeing concepts of the Gospel and
immunizes them
from the imprisonment and spiritual infirmities of the world at large.

So . . . . how?
How to get that Spirit and how to keep it?
Six suggestions:

First of all,
want it.
Those who have received the *gift* of the Holy Ghost
        following baptism
have the right
to the constant companionship of the third member
        of the Godhead . . . .
but the *right* is not deliverable on demand . . . .
He will draw closer to us as we do to Him.[1]
Free agency does not incorporate His uninvited or
        unappreciated presence.
Pray for his power.
God has promised his willingness to "visit" our marriages
with His power,
thus making a two-way weak partnership
into a three-way strong one.

---

[1]Doctrine and Covenants 88:63.

Second, a couple of "don'ts":
Don't quarrel in the home.
(Does that sound like an impossible admonition?)
Not really . . . . if you must quarrel, if this time the urge
    is irresistible,
leave the home . . . . fight it out elsewhere . . . .
pollute some atmosphere other than your own . . . .
(even if you're just in the car or the back yard.)
Also . . . .
never retire without a good feeling.
Clear the decks . . . .
expose the seeds of discontent . . . .
resolve them before going to sleep.
(You'll sleep a little better, and you'll wake up a lot better.)
Again, bring the third partner into the discussion
(through prayer) . . . .
With Him there, you'll work things out before you
lose very much sleep.

Third, be so aware of correct priorities
(family first, Church second, world third)
that frustrations from the third priority cannot have
much effect
on the first priority.
When you are physically home, be spiritually and mentally
    there also.
Bring the world in only when you wish to share it.
See things in their eternal perspective so that no
    momentary problem
is treated as a catastrophe.
Cultivate calmness and peace.

Fourth, since you have "the testimony of Jesus [which] is
the spirit of prophecy,"[1]
establish your home on the basis outlined for the
school of the prophets in the Doctrine and Covenants:
"Organize yourselves; prepare every needful thing; and establish
    a house,
even
a house of prayer,
a house of fasting,
a house of faith,
a house of learning,
a house of glory,
a house of order,
a house of God."[2]

Fifth,
Pray for your families and for your children[3] and recognize
that if you teach them correct principles,
they will govern themselves.[4]
Show full confidence in the Gospel . . . . teach your children that
it encompasses all truth . . . . and when a question comes
that you can't answer,
have faith that it can *be* answered, through study and
    through prayer.
Make your children open and broad . . . . encourage them
    to question
and to seek truth
rather than to accept things blindly.
A testimony is a gift that can't be given . . . . it can only
    be gained . . . .
but we can *give* our children the desire and the tools necessary
to *gain* one;

---

[1]Revelation 19:10.
[2]Doctrine and Covenants 88:119.
[3]Doctrine and Covenants 88:114.
[4]Joseph Smith.

and as we strive to build open, seeking minds, we are also giving
the capacity for great knowledge,
the capacity for tolerance toward others, and
the capacity for responsiveness and sensitivity to new truth
from any source.

Sixth, if you hold the priesthood,
use it
in your home to bless your family, to lead your family.
Don't wait for a crisis . . . . Is not a frightened child
or an exhausted wife
or a worried student
enough of a reason for a priesthood blessing?
Of course, it is; and the use of the priesthood will not only
have a direct effect on the immediate problem at hand . . . . it
will also unite a family spiritually in a way that cannot be
achieved otherwise,
and it will induce the humility and gratefulness
that permits the presence of the Holy Ghost.

Think about those six ways of attracting the proper spirit to
your home . . . . add whatever others you can think of,
and consider the possibility
that the Holy Spirit of Promise[1]
is essentially the final destination and the top rung
of a lifetime of Holy Ghost dependency and presence.

———
[1]Doctrine and Covenants 88:3-4; 132:26.

● 3. *The order of the family . . . .*
means its organization and direction and operation.
A family should not be a democracy
(even though some democratic characteristics are good).
A family should not be a dictatorship
(even though parents must have some elements of
        absolute authority).
A family should be a *patriarchal order,*
with the father as head,
committed to obey God in righteousness.
The wife's covenant is to obey her husband in righteousness.
Their collective commitment is to protect each other . . . .
to become one . . . .
and to accept the stewardship over others of God's children during
their early-earth stages.
The beauty of patriarchal covenants (husband to God and
wife to husband) is that they perfect the individuals
as well as the union . . . .
By obeying God, he leads her by the power and charisma
of righteousness rather than by coercion or demand;
and by obeying her husband, she keeps her own covenant and
demonstrates the faith and dependency that makes a man
strong
and that maximizes his chances of leading righteously.
Thus each protects the other,
and both increase their collective chance to return to God.

The "head of the family" role of the priesthood
and the "heart of the family" role of the wife
are very different,
but very equal . . . .
which is the very best way it could ever be . . . . because
carbon-copy roles create competition,
jealously, envy, insecurity, conceit, and
a narrowing of each individual . . . . while
differing and complementing roles create sharing,
interdependency, admiration, respect, and
a broadening of each individual.
We live in an age of specialization, and specialization can take no
more natural or sensible form
than the patriarchal order.

In addition to "role" order, we should also think about
"thing order," and
"thought order," and
"objective order."

"Thing order" affects the spirit of a home.
Having a place for things, and having things in those places,
saves time and aggravation . . . . and, somehow,
our minds unclutter as our environments unclutter.
When you put something away, you are putting a little love away
with it.
(Both for the one who uses it next and for the one who would have to
put it away if you didn't.)

"Thought order" and "objective order," in a family context,
mean setting goals and priorities
together.
Unity comes through commonality of purpose . . . . and a family
with the collective, clearly understood goal of
returning, together, to God . . . .
and with shorter range goals based on that great goal . . . .
will have a unity not ever found elsewhere; and will treat
each other
as the top priority that
each other
really is.

• 4. *Family pride and traditions.*
Both the word "pride" and the word "tradition" may have some
negative connotations
until the word "family" is put in front of them.
"Family pride" means to *identify* with one's family . . . . and to
     view one's
family
as the center of the universe.
The right kind of family pride gives children a feeling of belonging,
and produces a confidence and security
that allows them to face almost anything.

Family pride grows out of family traditions . . . . out of doing things
together,
and out of having family projects,
and family decisions,
and family secrets,
and family objectives,
and family habits,
and family jokes,
and family home evenings.
It is hard to imagine the value of family identity to a child.
If, in his mind, "what he is"
is first "a child of God" and second "a member of my family"
then he will have more inherent self-assurance than can be gained
anywhere else in the world.

Isn't it a fact that all great and venerable institutions
are built on and around traditions?

And is there any more important institution to you than your
family?
Traditions grow from the repetition of activities that you love.
For one family this may mean
Inviting a needy family on Thanksgiving,
or family competition and family "records" (Who can hold
      their breath longest?),
or family vacations to a special place,
or singing when everyone's together in the car,
or a Santa Claus suit for Dad on Christmas,
or going to see autumn foliage on an October birthday,
or a jack-o-lantern carving competition on Halloween.
It doesn't matter so much *what* they are . . . .
what matters is *that* they are.
Things to anticipate . . . . things to look forward to . . . . things to
depend on . . . .
consistent things in an inconsistent world.

In amongst the regularized, recurring family tradition, have
an occasional major family project.
Build a cabin together, or
plant a garden together, or
learn to water-paint together . . . .
anything . . . . together.

Abstract, unchanneled time together is better than none at all,
but not nearly as good as constructive, purposeful time together.
We learn to know others most quickly and most accurately
when we work with them
on common projects.

• Sharing, order, spirit, pride and tradition . . . .
we said four pillars . . . .
actually, they are better described as pieces
to the same puzzle.
Each one helps the other three to fit in.
"Family order" generates a calm spirit, a desire to share,
        a simple pride.
"Family sharing" expresses the spirit's love, and creates
        family traditions.
"Family spirit" results from and produces sharing and
        tradition and order.
"Family tradition" brings about family pride, and pride
        becomes the motivation
for spirit and order and sharing.

Strive to keep one thing foremost in your mind as you think
about family:
In Western countries, we sometimes feel so superior to,
        and have
pity for, those with less . . . .
and we conclude an enormous inequality and question the
fairness of God.
Let us not go so far in our judgments of inequality . . . .
because in fact
the essence of human experience . . . .
the source of real joy . . . .
is available to all people of all societies.
The experience of man-woman love and the
miracle of offspring, and the depths of feeling that go with each
are potentially present among all people
(and, in fact, stand the greatest danger of extinction
not among the primitive or the poor,
but among us).

Chapter 8

Oneness

Benjamin Franklin thought so much of
the institution of marriage
that he called a single person "the odd half of a pair of scissors."
And it's true . . . . it is simply true . . . . there is an incompleteness
about singleness . . . .
Not because of the mores of our society
or because of what we have become accustomed to,
but because
a man and a woman are this world's greatest example of a
mutual complement.
What a man is and what a woman is are
different
in an unalterable and mutually beneficial way.
All of the attempts to destroy or break down these
basic differences
will ultimately fail . . . .
and we should be glad, for it is these differences which provide
the world's greatest joy . . . .
and which permit the kind of merger that magnifies and develops
the strengths of each . . . .
and which forges bonds with a oneness that two "likes" could
never obtain.

To say that the roles of the man and of the woman are *different*
is *not* to say that they are unequal.

Who ever said that things must be the same in order to be equal?
Is the rain any more important to growth
than the soil?
Is the pitcher more essential to the baseball team
than the catcher?
Are the bricks a more important part of the wall
than the mortar?

If a tall, thin man and a short, strong man both pick apples
(from opposite sides of the same tree) . . . .
each picking his whole side,
each busheling his own,
each carrying his own to the truck . . . .
would the total result be as great as if
the tall man picked the high branches and the
strong man lifted the bushels to the truck?

To us who live in a society built around specialization,
should it be so difficult to acknowledge the
natural
and wonderful specialization that can exist in marriage?

The basic differences between man and woman date back beyond
this world,
and God established the patriarchal order of this earth
because of those differences.
The husband holds the priesthood and is the family's
head;

the wife supports and encourages and shares that priesthood,
       and is the
mother . . . . the consistent influence from within the home . . . .
she is the family's
heart.

But wait . . . .
wait.
The real message is not in the differences
or in the separateness . . . .
but in the oneness.
The word "synergysm" applies to a situation where two things
complement each other so well that the combined result
is actually greater
than the sum of its two parts.
Any kind of effective, coordinated teamwork
results in a degree of synergysm . . . .
and a strong marriage is
synergysm
in its purest form . . . . so pure that a better name is
oneness.
(Not the oneness of sheep, who lose their individuality
by following each other,
but the oneness of *purpose* . . . . the same oneness that Christ
wanted for his disciples when he asked of His Father,
"Make them one, as We are."[1]

---

[1]John 17:11.

Most marriages are like this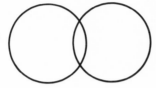

And they ought to be like this

● Now again, the recurring question . . . . how . . . .
how to achieve that oneness?
We have three suggestions:
1. Strive to communicate totally.
2. Strive to "out-give" each other.
3. Strive toward collectively set goals.

Two who do these three things . . . . are
one.

Still, again . . . . how?
(The question recurs, much like the child who says "Why?"
to the answer to his previous "Why?")
How to communicate?
How to out-give?
How to set mutual objectives?

Here are three suggestions for
how
to do each of the three:

● 1a. Communicate with your marriage partner by having a date
each week
on a set night
together
by yourselves
without friends
without children
alone
in a place where communication can happen.

If it's "been a while" since you've done this,
and you find yourselves getting to know each other all
      over again . . . .
don't be too surprised . . . .
just be glad.

1b. Communicate by listening.
Karl Rogers, renowned educator, developed the best
(and simplest) listening method, and called it
Rogerian technique.
It consists of simply repeating (in an interested and
      encouraging tone)
the essence of what someone says to you
(not asking, not directing, just listening and repeating
      in paraphrase).
As the talker sees that the listener is actually understanding
what he says,
he is prompted to go on . . . . and his mind charts its own course.
The destination of the discussion may surprise the talker as well
as the listener.
As much can be learned by talking to a pure listener

as by listening to a pure talker.
Try it and see.

1c.   Communicate by making an all-time, unequivocal commitment
to say
all
of what you *feel* . . . . to avoid the harboring of feelings inside.
The old adage that says "some things are better left unsaid"
is not true in marriage.
Oneness is achieved by saying all that is felt
(though "saying" can be done with or without words, and should
always be done in gentleness).

A man cannot be one with himself unless his outsides say
what his insides feel,
and he cannot be one with his wife until she knows the inside
as well as the outside.
A negative feeling, unsaid and held within,
will fester.
A positive feeling, unsaid and held within,
will never achieve its potential for joy.
It may be helpful to have a specific time . . . . a period
        set aside . . . .
when unsaid things get said.
Occasionally
take time to have a
private testimony meeting.
Bear testimony to each other
and of each other . . . .
say all that is inside to say, and close
in Christ's name.

● 2a. Out-give each other . . . .
The "out-giving game" is played by husband and wife . . . .
either player can initiate it, and
the other will inevitably follow.
Though it takes a lifetime to perfect the game,
beginners can often do surprisingly well.
The objective is to give more than you receive,
and there is no loser,
because when the game is played properly,
both players win.

A good way to initiate the game is to commit yourself
to doing one "window deed" each day for your spouse.
(Window reveal others and illustrate empathy . . . . as opposed to
mirrors which reflect the self and illustrate selfishness.)
The window deed might be an invitation to lunch,
or a half-hour alone while you take the children,
or a simple compliment,
or a rose,
or a neck rub at the end of a hard day,
or a love note in a lunch pail,
or a special appetizer at dinner,
or a breakfast in bed . . . .
Base your daily gift on need . . . . and watch your spouse
      close enough
to know what things bring delight.
Only if you know how she is
do you know what to give.
If you see fatigue, give rest,

if you see boredom, give excitement,
if you see drabness, give color . . . .
Make each window deed fit her present need.
Translate what you see in her
into what you give to her.
It's not easy to think of a window deed each and every day . . . .
but it's worth the time it takes . . . .
both through the joy you'll have in giving,
and through the gifts that will return to you.

2b.   Out-give each other by the exercise of
writing
a detailed "spouse description."
Describe your husband or wife physically, mentally, emotionally,
socially, spiritually.
Write it in the clearest and most graphic way that you can.
Be honest, but let your love seep through . . . . into the
description.
As you write, you will automatically multiply your
empathy . . . .
and you will increase your potential ability to help and to better
your partner . . . .
and you will find the adage, "We love those whom we know,"
to be true.
When you read your own description, written by your spouse,
you will improve your self-image . . . .
and you will come to understand yourself better . . . .
and you will find the adage, "We love those who know us,"
to be true.

Writing it will take a large amount of time and a larger amount of
thought,
but what you are giving here, to your husband or wife,
is no ordinary gift . . . .
It is the gift of a strong self-image,
and when you have given that
you have given confidence, and security,
and happiness.

2c.   Out-give each other by making a personal list
of two things:
"what she needs"
and
"what I must be to her."
Both will grow (to some extent) out of the "spouse description"
and both will help you to find a window deed
each day.

Once you have a "needs" list . . . . once you have personally
thought through
her needs for appreciation,
for support,
for time,
for confidence,
for interest,
for strength,
for spiritual nourishment,
for laughter,
etc., etc., ...

once you have summoned everything you know about her . . . . and
carefully pinpointed the unique needs . . . .
then *giving* will become easier, because you will know
what to give.
As you come to know more clearly what she needs
from you,
you will automatically know what you must *be*
to her.
List these things too, and let them
become
the "you" that you strive to
become.

When the two lists are made
(not "completed" because you will add to them as you know more)
put them in a personal place . . . . and take them out periodically
to read through
and to think through.
Don't begrudge the time it takes, for it will improve your
        performance
in your life's most important role.

• 3a. Set goals together on a yearly basis
   by taking one full day (out of every three hundred and
         sixty-five)
   to be alone together, to be away,
   and to decide where you'll be a year later.
   Oneness means one in purpose, and purpose means
   goals.
   Five-year goals and one-year goals are like puzzles
   within puzzles.
   The Gospel gives us the clear-cut outline of the
   puzzle board in which the pieces fit by telling us that our
   lifetime goal
   is to return to the presence of God.
   Without that puzzle outline, the various five-year pieces
   floating in front of us
   would be impossible to choose between.
   With the puzzle board of the lifetime goal, however, we have
   the potential to choose the pieces
   that fit our particular puzzle board, and that fulfill our individual
   foreordination.[1]
   Within each five-year piece are five one-year pieces.

   Each year, do two things:
   First, redefine where you want to be five years hence.
   Second, decide specifically what that means for the
   one year
   ahead.

   ───────
   [1]President Harold B. Lee, Conference Address, October 1973.

The process should work like a locomotive
on a seventy-mile night journey.
The headlight illuminates only a mile of track,
but,
when that mile is achieved, another mile
is lit.

The closer the goal, the more specific it should be.
A three-year goal of publishing a book may break into
one-year goals of
choosing and researching a topic,
producing a manuscript,
finding a publisher.

No one can teach you the incredibly valuable talent of
setting goals,
but you can learn the art
if you will follow four principles:
First, always start your thought process with the
longest-range goal and work back through
five-years,
one-year,
one-month,
and one-week counterparts.
(The repetitive thought on the long range will program your mind
and keep you on target in an almost automatic way.)
Second, write your goals down and make them specific enough that
they are measurable . . . . so that you know

(when the period is up)
whether you have fully achieved them.
Third, reassess and readjust your goals often.
(This is another reason for thinking through the long-range goals
all over again each time you sit down to plan.)
Even though the longest-range goal (returning to God) is constant,
you
and your circumstances
and your opportunities
are forever changing.
Fourth, set and readjust goals in partnership (in prayer)
with God . . . .
for only He can see the finished puzzle,
or the track's ultimate destination.

3b. Set goals together during an
"executive session" of family home evening.
After the closing prayer and after the children retire . . . .
reconvene . . . .
just the two of you . . . .
Evaluate the evening and evaluate the needs of each child
while they are fresh in your mind.
Then look at your five-year and one-year goals.
Once a month
break out collective monthly goals from the outline of the
yearly goals . . . .
and each week, plan the next week.
Write them.

Discuss them.
Commit to them.
Let it be a time when the king and the queen
counsel together
on the past, the present, and the future
of their kingdom
and of each of their subjects.

3c. Pursue goals together by making your daily prayers into
three-way partnership meetings
(attended by the heavenly Partner as well as by the two
earthly partners).
Discuss the goals with Him and ask for His help in their
readjustment and in their achievement.
Some men have suggested that we stay aware of our goals by
rehearsing them to ourselves each day while
looking into a mirror.
How much better it is to talk of them with God while
looking into heaven.

● Well . . . .
   you have just read three suggestions on
   how
   to achieve each of the three elements of "oneness" in marriage.
   Three times three is nine, and you may say
   it's complicated,
   and difficult,
   and time-consuming.
   But remember . . . .
   " . . . . no other success can compensate . . . . "
   " . . . . no other work is more important . . . . "
   Also,
   the fact of the matter is that the nine things are a joy
   and not a difficulty.

Once you have: (1) Set the five- and one-year goals,
                       (2) Written the "spouse description,"
                       (3) Written the "needs" and "what I must be"
                            documents . . . .
then a weekly schedule will achieve the other six:

Sunday	Monday	Tuesday	Wednesday	Thursday	Friday	Saturday
Daily "Spouse Window Deed"						
	Family Home Evening "Executive Session"				weekly "date"	
Daily "Three-Way Partnership Meeting"						

During the family home evening executive session:
> (4) The weekly goals are set and
> (5) Personal testimonies are born and all accumulating feelings are exposed and expressed.

On some set night later in the week:
> (6) The weekly "date" happens, and
> (7) The Rogerian technique has a chance to work.

Then, on a daily basis:
> (8) The "spouse window deeds" and
> (9) The three-way partnership meeting happens.

Now again, just to re-emphasize, these ideas can be
perfected, and individualized, and tailored, and revised,
and substituted for . . . .
until you believe that you have a program that will
create oneness
in *your* marriage.
The critical thing is that *you have* a program,
that it be *your* approach,
and that you work at it with the tenacity and determination
that is deserved
by the most important relationship in this world.

Any way you view it, the time spent and the effort rendered
is insignificant
in comparison with the benefits that accrue.

Chapter 9

Stewardship

- Sitting sideways in a little cafe, we looked out on the
    people-traffic
  of a large and busy shopping mall . . . .
  We noticed that adult passersby *never* looked at us
  and that children *always* did.
  (Every child did . . . . directly . . . . for at least a moment.)
  Is it any wonder that children learn so quickly and
  miss so little?
  If you watch them
  (as closely as they watch you)
  you will see that they see
  everything
  (and hear and smell and taste and feel).
  They are almost transparent . . . . data flows in from all directions
  and they are incredibly sensitive receivers.
  Thus as the child learns from the man,
  he teaches the man
  how to learn.

  Children know how to receive the data,
  but they don't know how to assimilate it,
  or understand it.
  We have the responsibility for these totally malleable,
  totally impressionable,
  totally influenceable
  beings;
  and within that responsibility lies our most important stewardship.

The earth and everything that is in it is God's,
and we are mere stewards
over what he has placed in our care.
Nowhere is that stewardship responsibility so great as with
our children . . . .
for their spirits exist eternally with ours, and we made
the decision to come to this earth
at the same time they did . . . .
in that pre-existent council
in heaven.
Because of the chronology and order of this earth, and because
of many factors that we don't fully understand,
we got here
twenty or thirty years before they did, and hence, they
(our spirit brothers and sisters)
come into mortality
as our children.
Thus they are dependent on us to teach and guide them
during the time before they can guide themselves.[1]

The choicest of God's spirit children
come to earth now,
in the last times . . . . in some ways the hardest of times . . . .
when all standards are questioned,
when all institutions are criticized,
and when the temptation of apathy, affluence and acceptance
replace the physical hardships that used to keep families
together.

---
[1]Doctrine and Covenants 68:25-28.

• So the responsibility of the stewardship is immense . . . .
but . . . .
as always . . . .
the magnitude of the responsibility
parallels
the magnitude of the reward.
Oh, just think for a moment about
children . . . .
How can we ever repay them for all that they
teach us
and for all the joy they bring!
If all things in the world were valued on the basis of
how much happiness they create . . . .
children
would head the list.
We watch their quick-lighting faces,
and feel the love in their arms
and in their eyes,
and we
learn from how they learn.
They come into the world and teach us the joys of
spontaneous delight,
of realness and honesty and candor,
of total receptivity and observation of environment,
of feeling and reacting openly to the spirit of calmness
(or to its opposite),
of open, overt love and trust,
of living in the present without overriding concern for past
        or future.

God said that "men are that they might have joy."
Our challenge, as parents, is to
preserve
and *protect*
these six joys with which our children are born.

In addition, we must *teach* them
the joys that *did not* enter with them . . . . the joys that they
were sent to this world to gain:
The joy of security,
The joy of confidence,
The joy of freedom of choice . . . . of making decisions
The joy of imagination and creativity,
The joy of work and physical activity,
The joy of being one's self and appreciating uniqueness,
The joy of a sense of humor,
The joy of sharing and loving others more than self,
The joy of family identity and pride,
The joy of learning and discovering new truth,
The joy of obedience to law,
The joy of man-woman love,
The joy of communication and relationships,
The joy of spiritual knowledge and testimony,
The joy of creating and of appreciating the created and
      the creative,
The joy of achievement and goal striving,
The joy of service and of being extra-centered,
The joy of understanding the depths of other people.

That makes six joys to learn from children and to
preserve
in them . . . . and at least
Eighteen joys to teach them . . . .
Quite a job,
but of all jobs, most rewarding. Rewarding both because
their joy is our joy
and
because we have need to learn most of the twenty-four
        joys ourselves.

• Think about what each joy entails . . . .
just think for a moment about each one . . . . and about what it takes
to teach it.

As you think,
we can fling some wide suggestions toward your mind,
but you will truly understand each joy (and how to teach it)
only through your own pondering . . . .
and your own prayer.

Here are some thought prompters:

Preserve the joy of spontaneous delight by sharing it.
Emote *with* your children; strive to feel the moment
as they do.

Preserve the joy of realness and honesty and candor
by emulating it,
by praising it when it surfaces most obviously.

Preserve the joy of total receptivity to environment by
watching what they watch
and by hearing what they hear (and what they say),
by emulating the alertness and sensitivity and by
encouraging the natural curiosity.
Teach children to glory in their wonderings . . . .
teach them that there is always a way to seek an answer . . . .
teach them that some questions have no answers, that others have
many answers . . . .

teach them how to fish rather than giving them a fish you've
    already caught.

Preserve the joy of feeling the Holy Ghost by including children
in family prayer (even at very young ages),
by using the priesthood more in the home,
by taking quarrels outside the house.

Preserve the joy of open, overt love,
by returning it
as physically and warmly as it is given,
show love for all living things . . . . have
pets and plants . . . .
and teach children the specialness of things which
are co-eternal with us (God, this earth, other people,
    and animals).
Preserve a child's trust in adults by being truthful with him
even in small things.
(Don't say, "The doctor won't hurt you.")

Preserve the joy of living in the present by
being there
with your children . . . . and by forgetting (at least for
    joyous moments)
both yesterday
and tomorrow.

• Teach the joy of security
by consistency and equality in example and in discipline
and by making the home a sanctuary of unconditional love.

Teach the joy of confidence by recognizing unique gifts
and by explaining the ultimate power
of faith in God.
Give children a good reputation by
simply telling them
that they are good, that they are important, that they are capable,
that they are bright.
Children will be what they think they are,
and what they think they are is almost entirely a product
of what *you* think they are.

Teach them the joy of freedom
by giving it to them . . . .
and the joy of making decisions
by letting them make them.
(Children who are given the latitude to make their own decisions
early,
before the consequences of wrong choice are too severe,
will learn how to decide before they reach the age where wrong
decisions produce serious and sometimes unalterable consequences.)
Show children correct principles
and they will govern themselves.
Show them truth, and watch that truth make them free.[1]

---

[1] John 8:31-32.

Teach them the joy of imagination and creativity
by acting out stories with them,
by helping them paint and dance,
by encouraging and reinforcing each imaginative and creative
thread that shines through,
and by becoming a child with them
every chance you get.

Teach them the joy of physical activity
by roughhousing with them while they are young,
and teach them the joy of hard work
by working shoulder to shoulder with them when they are older.
Teach them the joy of working together as a family unit
by having family projects
(anything from building a summer home to planting a garden).

Teach them the joy of being themselves and of being unique
by *showing* them that they *are* unique
and by convincing them that their unique gifts are as good
and as valuable as anyone else's.
Encourage and appreciate each talent or ability you get a
        glimpse of.
Teach young children to say "I am" and to value and defend their
free agency and their power to choose.
Teach them by telling them (repetitively) that they are
unique in all the world.
Never destroy a child's fragile self-image by belittling him . . . .
instead . . . .
talk with facts.

Instead of saying, "Don't play in your food, you big baby,"
say, "You're too young to eat in this restaurant; soon you'll be
older and able to control your spoon and fork better."

Teach the joy of a sense of humor
by laughing with your children . . . . and by helping them to
laugh at themselves and at their own mistakes.
Help them to see that "apparent crisis plus time equals humor."

Teach them the joy of sharing and loving others more
        than themselves
by loving *them* more than *yourself;* and by using the
"interest book" idea,
and the "round table" idea,
and the "favorite-things wall" idea that were
mentioned earlier;
and by showing your emotional affection
in a physical way.

Teach them the joy of family identity and pride and excellence
by talking about "the family" often,
and by connecting any achievement by any individual in the family
to the family;
and by having the kind of family traditions mentioned on
        page 100.

Teach them the joy of listening and of discovering truth
by exploring with them,
and by paying attention to all people,
and by using clear logic with them even when they are
very young.

Teach them the joy of obedience to law
by demonstrating the law of the harvest . . . . by allowing them
to reap the negative consequences of minor broken laws.
Emphasize obedience to law rather than obedience to people.
("Because I told you so" is never a very good answer.)
Teach children to understand the difference between
thoughts and actions . . . .
teach them that it is all right to have scary feelings or
        mad feelings . . . .
that they are natural . . . . that everyone has them . . . .
        that they are things to be controlled and not things
        to be ashamed of.

Teach them the joy of man-woman love by
letting them see *your* man-woman love . . . . by hand-holding
        and hugging,
by sitting next to each other and a kiss as you leave.
Let them see it physically and mentally . . . .
avoid any harsh word in their presence, and remember the
wise phrase that goes, "The best thing a man can do for his
children is to love their mother."

Teach them the joy of communication and relationships
by always having time to talk . . . .
by being real and genuine and by acting mad when you're mad
and sad when you're sad . . . .
by speaking candidly and logically and graphically . . . .
and by making the first relationship of their lives
(the one with you)
a high standard for all others to reach and a relationship
where what is *felt* is what is *said.*

(If a child relates well enough to you to say, "You scare me
when you yell," the chances are good that he will relate
well enough to his teacher to say, "I'm just so worried that I
can't get it right.")

Teach them the joy of spiritual knowledge and testimony
by showing full confidence in the Gospel . . . .
and in the answers it contains.
Have frequent family testimony meetings
as part of family home evenings.

Teach them the joy of creating and of appreciating the creative
        and the created,
by sharing the wonder in
a snow-capped mountain or in
a simple poem . . . .
and by welcoming every small creative effort on their part
as though it was
the unveiling of a masterpiece.

Teach them the joy of achievement and goal-striving
by having family goals
which are worked toward and met,
and by having an individual yearly goal-setting session with them
each year,
just as you do with each other.
Teach them not to fear failure . . . . to see it not as a disgrace,
but as a necessary part of growing.
Teach them that needing the help of others is not weakness
        but a blessing.

Teach them the joy of service and of being
extra-centered
by doing good turns with them . . . . in secret . . . .
(inside and outside the family),
Watch the joy that the deeds produce, and discuss it with them.
Explain that they are one in one thousand with the fulness
of the Gospel . . . .
and make them understand the related meaning of, "Where much
is given, much is expected."[1]

Teach them the joy of understanding others by telling them
why people act as they do . . . . "The reason that little boy feels bad
is that his mother yelled at him a few moments ago."
Arm your child with understanding, so he'll know why others
(and himself)
are sometimes angry or mean or rude.
Teach children that things are not always black and white . . . .
that complex questions sometimes don't have simple answers . . . .
"Maybe Bill took something that didn't belong to him because
he was poor and hungry."
Don't be unrealistic about the world . . . . let children see
human imperfection,
and explain it to them as best you can.

---

[1]Doctrine and Covenants 82:3.

● Isn't it interesting that all the joys are taught
to children
by experiencing them
with children . . . .
As we teach and give joy,
we learn and receive joy.

Now that we have talked about *what* we should strive to teach
our children, and tried to dissect and examine each of them a bit,
let's look at the methods by which children learn,
and consequently
the methods by which we can teach them.

Parents teach children by
setting example, by
setting law, by
setting environment, by
setting knowledge, and by
setting tone.
Let's think about each one for a moment.

- *Setting Law* (Children learn by obeying and by deciding)
  A family is an institution and,
  like any institution,
  it must have laws and operating procedures.
  By having them, it teaches children to be a positive part of
  a successful family, and it prepares children
  for other laws . . . .
  laws of this country and of this universe.
  At a very early age, children should be taught the difference
  between their parents' *laws* (things in which obedience
      will be enforced)
  and
  their *parents' desires* (areas where parents will counsel and give
  advice but where the child must make his own decisions).
  Set up a list of "family laws" . . . .
  a small number of absolutes . . . . built around personal safety
  and the rights of others.
  Write them down and treat them as simple, clear facts of life
  with automatic and immediate punishment for violation.
  Children find great security in absolutes . . . . in consistency . . . .
  And though the punishment will be unpleasant,
  it will also be (if it is consistent) a source of security and of
  identification with the family institution.

  Where these absolutes or family laws are concerned,
  tell your children.
  Where the nonabsolutes are concerned,
  ask and *advise* your children.

When a child comes to you and asks you to make a decision
      for him . . . .
don't do it (unless it is answered by a law).
Instead, do as Heavenly Father does with us . . . .
ask him to study it out, to make his own best decision, and
to come back to you to discuss that decision and to get a
confirmation
that it is the right decision.[1]

A family that operates this way (laws governing things that
must be governed, advice and free agency on things that don't)
doesn't have to deal in threats,
or bribery
as so many families do . . . .
Rather, it deals simply with laws
and with decisions,
which are the two basic ingredients that make up a life,
and that make up this world.
A child who learns that obeying laws makes him free,
and who learns *how* to make decisions in "nonlaw" situations,
has learned the very essence of successful living.

---

[1]Doctrine and Covenants 9:7-9.

● *Setting example* (Children learn by watching)
 If you say:
 "I want children who are well-rounded, who are open and honest,
 who can earn their own way and have a happy marriage and a
 service-oriented life" . . . .
 then the most reliable method is:
 To *be* well-rounded, open and honest; to work hard to build a
 good home and a solid orientation to service.
 Example . . . .
 it is the strongest teacher.
 The only time it doesn't work is when some other example
 is stronger
 or when a child doesn't believe in himself completely enough
 to follow.

● *Setting Environment* (Children learn by experiencing)
A great mother once surrounded her baby's crib with
sights and sounds and stimulations
for all five senses.
A great father once required his children to report
(each night before dinner)
on one of the editorials from that day's *New York Times*.
Both were setting an environment of stimulation . . . .
Both were teaching their children *how* to learn.

A bored child is as seriously deprived as an undernourished one.

A major university
(knowing that more than 50 percent of intelligence is gained
     by age four)
set out to discover the reasons for the I.Q. differences
among elementary school children . . . .
children from similar incomes and demographic background.
They were looking for childhood differences between the "A"
children (high I.Q.) and the "C" children (low I.Q.).
They went back a year at a time.
Finally, when they got to the two-year-old and one-year-old levels,
they found the difference.
It was a difference in mothers.
The "A" mothers didn't spend any more time with their babies
than the "C" mothers,
but they allowed more freedom . . . . they let their children roam
throughout the house, they set up a dynamic environment
with sensory stimulation of all kinds,

They set up teaching situations and they spoke in adult tone
and language.
They encouraged curiosity and rewarded inquiry with answers.
The "C" mothers overprotected, put children in confining
        playpens,
worried too much about absolute cleanliness and safety,
and generally restricted their child's environment.
The researchers concluded that by the time children are
        eighteen months old or so,
"A" or "C" patterns are becoming set.

Children feel the Spirit of the Holy Ghost (and its opposite)
more clearly,
and probably more accurately
than we.
They hear and see love (and hate) distinctly, even when they are
vague to us.
So,
when all is said, and after all the theory is presented,
it is the calmness children feel, the spirit and love and atmosphere
of their environment,
that really counts.

● *Setting Knowledge* (Children learn by being verbally taught)
The most valuable information any human being can gain
is answers to questions about
beginnings
and purposes
and destinations.
We can teach the Gospel's answers to those questions to very
small children,
and thus fulfill the profound admonition
of Doctrine and Covenants 68:25-28.

Perhaps the real key to the verbal teaching of children
lies in the ability to teach them
when they want to learn
and *what* they want to learn.
The moments when children ask questions are precious because
their minds are open.
A parent who watches his children (with the objective of
     sensing what
it is that the child is thinking . . . . what he is wondering about . . . .
what he is curious about . . . . what he is open to . . . .)
will find many more teaching moments and will teach much
more effectively
than the parent who tries to teach what *he* wants to teach when
he wants to teach it.

● *Setting Tone* (Children learn by feeling)
 Teaching happens best
 when positive reigns over negative and
 calmness over tension and
 free will over coercion and
 questions over statements and
 talk of "what to do" over talk of "what not to do."

 Make your home a Gospel home (thou shalt love)
 rather than a Pharisaic home (thou shalt not . . . .)

 Be calm in all situations, big or small.

 Always ask children the question instead of telling them
      the answer.
 (That way *you* just might learn something . . . . you'll almost
 certainly learn that they knew more than you thought they did.)

• Perhaps most of what has been said in the last several pages
can be summarized by talking briefly
about two things that we would all want to give to
our children.
First, uniqueness and confidence as an individual child of God.
Second, pride and unity as a member of a family.

In order to give the first, we must get to know our children
as individuals.
It is so easy to make the great and common mistake
of trying to mold children into what we want them to be instead
of listening and observing what they really are.
We teach them what we want to teach
rather than what they want to learn,
and instead of finding and sharpening the individuality
and uniqueness
that *is* there,
we submerge it and dull it and try to build on something which
may be in our minds rather than in *their* spirits.

Some would say "an apple is an apple."
Yet did you know that you can get to know an individual apple
(even when blindfolded)
just by feeling it and concentrating on it . . . .
you can get to know it so distinctively that you can pick it
out
of a whole bushel of the same variety.
Now . . . .
some would say "a kid is a kid" . . . .

In order to get to know someone, you must spend individual time
with him.
Different types of parents might choose different ways of doing
      this with children.
One parent might choose the Rogerian technique described in an
earlier chapter
(which, incidentally, works amazingly well with small children).
Another might set up a regular system of
private interviews
where the child could ask or talk about whatever he wished.
Another might give a gift of
a half-hour
each day to each child . . . . a half-hour in which
      the child is *first* . . . .
before phone calls,
before the newspaper,
before anything . . . .
and where the two (parent and child) will do whatever the
child
wants
(for the full half-hour).
Another might have a weekly "daddy date" with a child . . . .
again where the child chooses where to go, what to see.

Whatever technique you like,
have one
and implement it consistently . . . .
Only if you do will you learn who your child
really is
and what he
really needs.

- As you come to know each little spirit that is
  sent to you . . . . you should
  check your perceptions often with those of your spouse.
  During the "executive session" of your family meeting,
  discuss each child individually . . . .
  What stage is he in?
  What achievements are there to recognize and reinforce?
  What uniqueness is there to magnify and draw out?
  What problems are developing, and how can you
  nip them
  in the bud?

The more you know about a child, the more you can
respect and admire him,
and the more genuine, positive reinforcement you can give.

Praise progress and achievement openly,
and explain *why* it is good and *what* the resulting benefits will be.

The strength you give a child by building him
as an individual,
will be magnified even further by the security and belonging
that he will feel as a part of a great family.
The family projects and traditions,
the family spirit and tone,
the family goals and order,
the family communication and sharing,
(all mentioned earlier)
will all help,

but it is the *love* in a family that forms the real bond.
It is the pat on the head,
the pleased, proud look,
the warm smile
that can turn a home into a sanctuary against the world,
and it is love
that serves life as the stem of a water lily serves the lily . . . .
by holding it within a certain set radius,
no matter
how the winds and torrents of the world
blow and pull away.

PART III

Relationships ...with God

"*And this is life eternal, that they might know thee the only true God, and Jesus Christ, whom thou hast sent.*"

Chapter 10

Knowing and Loving

The first part of this book (Relationships with Self)
and the second part of this book (Relationships with Family)
can never be fully and successfully attained
(or even completely understood)
without the last part of this book (Relationships with God).
Many have recognized this relationship among relationships.
H. G. Wells said:
"Until man has found God, and has been found by God, he begins
at no beginning and walks to no end. Nothing in the universe or
in man's life falls into place except with God."
Henry Martyn Field said:
"There is no brotherhood of man without the fatherhood of God."

No wonder, then, that God tells us through His scripture
that life eternal
is to "know God."[1]
As with so many scriptures, those two words have
multiple meanings:
Know God's existence and trust it;
Know God's love and reciprocate it;
Know God's will and live it . . . .
But in addition to all these aspects of knowing,
the scripture in its most basic and profound interpretation
simply means to get to know God as

---

[1] John 17:3.

a person . . . .
as you would a friend, as you would an earthly companion,
and perhaps *most* similarly
as you would your father.

The reward for building any relationship is the continuation
of that relationship
and of its benefits,
throughout eternity.
The reward for building a relationship with God, therefore,
reaches unimaginable proportions,
for continuation of a relationship with Him throughout eternity
means attainment of the celestial kingdom and eternal life.
And naturally it should be so, for to truly know God
is to truly love God,
and to love God is the first and great commandment[1]
which entails all other obedience,
and which insures the highest eternal reward.

---

[1]Matthew 22:37.

● The first thing involved in knowing anyone
is to know who he is and what he is.
The central purpose of the Gospel is to teach us who God is
and what He is
so that we can know Him,
and emulate Him.

It is through knowing the Gospel that we know God;
It is through knowing God that we know the Gospel.

Let's review the truths *we do know* of our relationship with God:
We know that we are God's offspring,[1]
that He is literally the Father of our spirits.[2]
(Of all the names that God could have chosen to be called . . . .
of all the titles He deserves . . . .
it is interesting that He chose "Father."
Of all the churches that address God by that title,
it is interesting that only one teaches that He is
actually and literally our spirit Father.)

We know that we lived with God in a pre-earthly existence
and shouted for joy[3] in that great council where our Father gave us
the opportunity to experience
(as He had)
an earthly existence with a physical body.[4]

---

[1] Acts 17:28.
[2] Hebrews 12:9; Romans 8:16-17.
[3] Lorenzo Snow, *Deseret Weekly*, 20:597.
[4] Joseph Smith, *Times & Seasons*, August 15, 1844.

We know that Jehovah,
the firstborn of God's spirit children and thus our Elder Brother,[1]
willingly accepted the Father's
proposed plan of salvation and free agency in the world that
    was to come,
and offered to come into that world
and atone
for the errors that He (and the Father) knew we would make.
We know that one-third of our Father's spirit children
used their *pre-mortal* free agency to vote against *earthly*
     free agency,
thus forfeiting their mortal opportunity
and departing with Lucifer
who had proposed an alternative plan of coercion and force.[2]

We know, partly because of our own parenthood,
that our Father mourned the loss of the one-third . . . .
and that it was with great concern that he sent the rest of us here.
(When parents send a son or daughter away to college, they do so
knowing
of the temptations there,
of the danger there,
of the possibility of failure there . . . .
Yet they also know that the child's growth is
limited
while living with the parent.)
Similarly . . . . God knew . . . . similarly God sent us.

---

[1] Doctrine and Covenants 93:21-23.
[2] Moses 4:1-4; Abraham 3:27-28.

We know that our tangible bodies are in the image
of God's tangible body;
and we know that if the veil were rent and we saw our
Heavenly Father today,
we would see Him as a man, with a tangible (though perfect and
unlimited) physical body.[1]

We know that the first begotten Son of God in the spirit
became the only begotten Son of God in the flesh . . . .[2]
that he *did* atone . . . .
that our salvation and eternal life are dependent on His grace,
after all we can do.[3]

We know that it is "no robbery of God"[4] to think of man
as being of the same species . . . .
and we know that, "As God is, man may become."[5]
This thought does not insult God . . . . it elevates man
        . . . . it gives
man confidence as he glimpses his potential.
If we equated ourselves more with God and less with beasts,
we would behave more like God and less like beasts.

---

[1] Joseph Smith, *Times & Seasons*, August 15, 1844.
[2] B. H. Roberts, *The Gospel, an Exposition of its First Principles
        and Man's Relationship to Deity* (Salt Lake City, Deseret Book Company,
        1928), pp. 292-294.
[3] 2 Nephi 25:23-26.
[4] Philippians 2:6.
[5] Joseph Smith, *Times & Seasons*, August 15, 1844.

We know that God is real . . . .
that He does have a body,[1]
that He does have parts,[2]
that He does have passions.[3]

We know that the Holy Ghost is the third member of the Godhead;
that He is separate and distinct from the Father and from the Son;
that as a spirit He has the mission to reveal and verify God to man;[4]
that He has the special commission and
power to teach truth to our spirits.

We know that God operates by natural law,
and we know that it is his omniscience of all natural law
that makes Him omnipotent.
His commandments to us, therefore, are not arbitrary,
        personal rules,
but loving counsel from a wise Father,
laws of life which He Himself keeps and uses and benefits from.

We know that we can have a real and personal
relationship with God.
Enoch and God related to each other as *friends,*
they shared in sorrow for the world,
and Enoch learned of God's concern for all His children firsthand
when he saw Him weep for the earth's inhabitants.[5]

---

[1]Genesis 1:26-27; Exodus 33:9-11, 21-23.
[2]Numbers 12:8.
[3]Jeremiah 44:4; 4:8; Exodus 20:5; 34:6; John 3:16.
[4]John 16:13.
[5]Moses 7:26-30.

● Knowing, as we do, that there are three distinct members
of the Godhead forces the question . . . .
Which do we strive to know?
Which do we pray to?

The question is, in a way, academic
because the Father-Son sameness is exact,
and to know one is to know the other.[1]
(And it is the similar Spirit of the Holy Ghost that testifies
of both.)

The question, in another way, has a definite and very useful
answer:
We must strive to know Jesus Christ
because He is Jehovah, the Creator of this world;[2]
because He is the Mediator between us and the Father;[3]
because He is our Savior on whom we are dependent for salvation
     and eternal life;[4]
because He will be our judge;[5]
because the scriptures are primarily about Him;
because His importance is such that the Father Himself
     came to earth to announce Him;
because no one goes to the Father except by the Son;[6]
because, since Christ is the Creator, the atoner and the judge
of this world, we are to be, in a way, His sons and daughters
as well as His brothers and sisters.

---

[1]John 14:7-9.
[2]Genesis 1:26; Ether 3:15-16; John 1:3.
[3]1 Timothy 2:5.
[4]3 Nephi 11:14; 1 Corinthians 15:22; Romans 3:23-25.
[5]John 5:22.
[6]John 14:6; 3:16.

(Every ordinance relates to this adoption process . . . .
in baptism we are born of Him . . . .
in the sacrament of His supper we reaffirm our taking
       His name and remember
His flesh-and-blood sacrifice . . . .
in the Gospel, we learn the full, eternal connection.)

So it is Jesus Christ whom we must strive to know . . . .
partly because it is He whom the Father has told us to know,
partly because it is He whom we can read of and learn of,
and partly because it is by knowing Him that we can come to know
the Father.

As we strive toward the knowledge of Christ,
and consequently of the Father,
the Holy Ghost will teach us what cannot be learned elsewhere,
and we will learn to know the Teacher as well as His topic . . . .
Ultimately, when the Spirit of the Holy Ghost becomes strong
enough to make our calling and election sure,
we will know Jesus Christ
well enough
that He will become our Second Comforter.[1]

Christ gave the answer to the second part of the
       earlier question . . . .
Who to pray to:
"Pray to the Father in my name."[2]
So we address our prayers to the Father, and we close in
Christ's name . . . .

---

[1] John 14:18-23; *Teachings of the Prophet Joseph Smith*, pp. 150-151.
[2] 3 Nephi 18:19.

Yet the prayer is to both . . . .
the oneness of the Father and the Son allow it to be so.
Pray to the Father but visualize two listeners . . . .
two in person . . . . but one in purpose and objective and judgment,
and one in
the answering of your prayers.

We are intensely interested in knowing about those we love,
and we usually come to love those about whom we learn
        a great deal.
Which starts the other is immaterial as long as both happen
with God.
It is paradoxical that so many spend lifetimes learning some
protracted field of
earthly knowledge . . . .
and, simultaneously, spend little or no time learning
Gospel truths
of eternal worth.

One way to know about the Lord is to
know scriptures. In them,
we can walk in His shoes and empathize with His life
and death.
Scriptures are hard to read only in the sense that anything
in which we have only vague interest is hard.
Scriptures are easy to read when interest is keen.
One does not learn Christ's life and nature because of some
"scripture-reading system" . . . .
he learns it because he has a desire . . . . a burning thirst to know.

(Systems are not inherently bad . . . . but they produce results
only when coupled with genuine desire.)

Another way to know about God is to
ask others who know Him.
If you perceive that a man has a good relationship with God,
ask him about it . . . .
find out what he knows and,
even more importantly,
find out how he found it out.

We can know the Father by understanding the
parallels between His parenthood and ours.
(One who is Parent, and who deeply wants to be a good parent,
can more easily come to know the greatest Parent.)
Incidentally, this particular coin has two sides . . . .
Just as being a good parent helps one to know God better,
so knowing God better (as a parent)
helps one to be a better parent himself.

• A testimony of God, like any relationship, is not an object, it
is not something that you either have or don't have.
Rather, it is constantly changing and never static.
It is, in fact,
always either waxing or waning to some degree . . . .
and the "waxing" of a testimony requires study and prayer
and commitment (whether you are first glimpsing God or
        continuing a long
and already close relationship with Him).
Perhaps we should more often say
"I'm knowing"
rather than
"I know"
for "testimony" is not a destination, but a journey
(in which consistent reevaluation and recommitting are essential).

You will begin to see Him (or is "feel" a better word?)
in your mind's eye . . . .
just as you mentally see anyone about whom you know a great deal.

The things He *did* tell you that He must have been strong
(physically as well as in other ways).
The things He *preached* tell you that He must have known great joy
(as well as great sorrow and concern and unparalleled charity).
The things He *promised tell* you how much He knew and how much
He controls.
(We call it omniscience and omnipotence.)

Be sure that what you learn about Him comes from Him
and not from the notions of others
or from the unreliable source of what your own mind
wants to believe.
Nothing falsifies and belies a relationship more quickly
than false assumptions and inaccurate impressions.
No two relationships are the same . . . .
yours cannot be patterned after any other,
nor can any other (or this book) explain precisely
what *your* relationship with God should be like.

If you form a genuine relationship with the true God,
that relationship
will be unique in all the world.

• There must be a distinction made between
knowing about God
and knowing God.
A list of statements *about* God is no more analogous
to a *relationship* with God
than is the study of Napoleonic history to a relationship
       with Napoleon.

So the all-important question of how . . . .
how to develop a true relationship with the true God . . . .
is still unanswered.

You'll remember that we made an earlier list . . . . of
       the components
of a "horizontal relationship" (mortal to mortal).
(back on pages 6 and 7)
Should that list apply . . . . does it apply . . . .
to a "vertical relationship" (mortal to immortal . . . . man to God)?

Yes.
They *do* all apply . . . .
for they are criteria for knowing people . . . .
and God is a person.
(And "man and God" can be perfectly translated into
       "son and Father".)
Oh, how important it is to view the difference between
       man and God
as a difference in *degree,*
and not
as a difference in *kind!*
The vertical relationship is in the same *plane* as the horizontal . . . .
the *species* is the same on each end of both relationships.

The component list, item by item, does apply . . . .
strikingly . . . .
to a relationship with God . . . . in fact, it sometimes applies more
clearly and more precisely there than to any other relationship.
Take a look at the list . . . .
(with Gospel-oriented synonyms added in parentheses)
and see if you don't agree.

Investment of time together . . . . (prayer)
Trust . . . . (faith)
Openness . . . . (real intent)
Honesty . . . . (truth)
Shared experience . . . . (Gospel service)
Background knowledge . . . . (scripture)
Personality insight . . . . (Gospel insight and knowledge)
Respect . . . . (reverence)
Interest . . . . (devotion)
Concern . . . . (testimony)
Admiration . . . . (worship)
Commonality . . . . (righteousness)
Commitment . . . . (obedience)
Giving of the self . . . . (consecration)
Empathy . . . . (compassion)
Understanding . . . . (enlightenment)
Communication . . . . (inspiration and prayer)
Patience . . . . (long-suffering and persistence)
Love . . . . (love)
Sincerity . . . . (sincere heart)
Delight . . . . (joy)

Participation . . . . (Church assignments)
Challenge . . . . ("As God is . . . . ")
Stimulation . . . . (revelation)
Progression . . . . (perfection)
Tolerance . . . . (charity)
Listening . . . . (guidance, inspiration)
Receiving . . . . (thankfulness for all)
Sharing . . . (sacrifice)

You see . . . . they all fit . . . .
As in any relationship, the greater the presence
of these components,
the stronger the relationship will be.

Each of the relationship components
could be probed to a far greater depth.
"Time spent together," for example, means so much
      in this relationship.
It is impossible *not* to know someone pretty well
after spending a considerable amount of time together . . . . and
our Heavenly Father is no exception
(particularly when you realize that getting to know Him is
not a first-time acquaintance, but the *renewing*
of a relationship
that existed before this world did).
The best kind of "time spent together," in any relationship,
is time spent working with someone on *their work* and
      their interests.
Nowhere is this more applicable than with God . . . .
for when we work
together with Him

on His work
He fills us with His Spirit, and we become one with Him.

Pages could be written on the applicability of each component . . . .
but rather than *reading* it,
why don't you *think* it . . . .
Take five minutes on each component and on what it means
in terms of your relationship with your Heavenly Father.
There are twenty-nine of them . . . .
It most likely will be the best and most beneficial
two hours and twenty-five minutes
you have ever spent.

● Easiest to love are those who have done much for us . . . .
who have given great gifts.
How easy, then, to love God . . . . and the Lord . . . .
who have given us:
Our mortal lives,
this earth and all that is in it,
loving counsel (commandments),
resurrection and eternal life,
salvation and potential exaltation,
the greatness and perfection of the plan of free agency,
and,
the fulness of the Gospel . . . .
which fills with love all who grasp it,
which draws us like a magnet to light and truth, and
to the higher realm of giving all for Christ as He did
for us;
Which makes "charity's" true definition, "the pure love of Christ";
and which makes the first and great commandment
inclusive
of all the others.

Chapter 11

Asking and Listening

• Just as we cannot know an earthly acquaintance through
  superficial conversation,
  so also we cannot know God through vain repetition or through the
  one-way monologue
  of talking but not listening.

Perhaps that notion should be stated even more strongly:
Just as superficial, insincere conversation creates distrust
and bad feeling in earthly relationships,
so also do our habitual, repetitive, parrot-like speeches to God
falsify and undermine and throw off course
any true relationship with Him.

Again, earthly examples illustrate important points . . . .
Would you approach an interview with some great man, someone of
importance and power in this world,
without some preparation,
without some thought?
And after asking him the question of your intent, would you hastily
leave the room . . . .
without waiting for his answer?
How then can we approach the Creator of the universe
as casually as we often do?
And how can we leave our knees after we've finished talking
but before we've started listening?

It's true that we are His children, and in that sense we are
        more important
than His other creations . . . .
but that parental relationship should increase our
respect and reverence,
not diminish it.

To all those who believe in a personal and loving God,
prayer has the potential of being an interview with a great Father,
a dialogue
where the spoken prayer is answered by the promptings of
        the Spirit
and the whisperings of inspiration.

Prepare before prayer.
Listen after prayer.
Both notions are as absolutely logical
as they are uncommonly practiced.

Learn from little children.
They are real and open, honest and genuine . . . .
and (unless we teach them our pat phrases and vain repetitions)
their prayers are simple and beautiful.
Christ not only loved little children . . . .
He told us to be like them;
and nowhere is that counsel better applied than in prayer.
Talk to the Lord as directly and as specifically as you would
to a friend.
A child who wants to know the product of two times six
asks for the product of two times six,

not for a general introduction to multiplication;
yet we,
wanting to know specific answers to specific problems,
ask for general "guidance."
(Incidentally, the wise father would tell his child to
work out two times six as well as he could and to
bring his answer back for right or wrong confirmation . . . .
and that
is exactly what the Lord asks us to do in the ninth section
of the Doctrine and Covenants.)

• Of all scriptural admonitions, none is mentioned more often
  and none is more consistently connected to an
          accompanying promise
  than the one-word admonition
  "ask."
  It is always followed by the four-word promise
  "and ye shall receive."

When we love someone fully, our inherent desire is to give,
and, therefore,
to long to be *asked*.
So it must be with God . . . .
for He asks us to ask Him.

The scriptures imply a definite cause-and-effect relationship
between asking and receiving,
But the concept of asking
is not complete
without the aspect of *persistence*.
Is an important request on this earth ever asked in one
isolated moment . . . .
without follow-up, without earnestness and tenacity?
Scripture is replete with examples of rewarded persistence . . . .
The woman who clutched the garment of Christ
until he focused on her and on her request;[1]
Christ's own parable of the friend knocking at the door
at midnight . . . . first put off by the master of the house
        . . . but
finally, through his persistence, rewarded;[2]

---

[1] Mark 7:25-30.
[2] Luke 11:5-8.

Enos, who persisted all day and all night in mighty prayer,
and who finally received a dramatic answer;[1]
Paul who simply told the Thessalonians to
"pray without ceasing."[2]
Extreme persistence is almost a demand . . . . a legitimate demand
for the fulfilling of the
cause-and-effect law of asking and receiving.
(The strength and persistence of prayer is better called
"faith"
than
"presumption"
because the divine promise is of an *answer* . . . .
not always the answer we want, perhaps, but nonetheless
       an *answer*.)

---

[1]Enos 3-18.
[2]1 Thessalonians 5:17.

• If we agree that God fulfills His promises, and if we recognize
the asking and receiving promise
as unequivocal . . . .
then the only possible reason for a nonanswer
is some failure in the asking.
There are three essential elements in asking from God
(and, therefore, three potential failures):
Faith,
Real intent and
Sincerity.[1]

Many would say that the first is hardest . . . . even to the point
of anachronism (having faith as you ask for faith).
Faith *is* hard,
but it is also simple because it has only two ingredients:
Desire,
and Evidence.
The desire is potentially in the breast of every man.
Scripture tells us that we are all born with the "light of Christ" . . . .
with a conscience . . . . with an inherent capacity to look and reach
upward.
Learning of Christ and *wanting* to know Him can kindle
      and fan this
light,
which burns at some level in every man.
One who is genuinely seeking to know soon realizes that
if there is a God,
and if He is what we call Him . . . . Father . . . .
then He would not give His children a stone when they
      ask for bread.[2]

---

[1]Moroni 10:4.
[2]Luke 11:11.

Realizing this, it is possible to exert a certain kind of faith
while praying for another (more complete) kind of faith.
The first prayer may be, "God, if thou dost exist, help me to
learn and know of that existence."

Along with desire, there must be some element of *evidence*
or at least a degree of
rational reason for believing in the possibility of a Supreme Being.
This evidence surrounds us:
The perfect design of a universe that must have had a designer;
The "first-time familiarity" with some people and places that leads
us to believe that we've known them in another, earlier time;
The coming forth of certain scripture and prophecy that
cannot be explained without belief in a Supreme Being;
The testimonies of great men . . . . great by any secular or
religious measurement . . . . who unequivocally claim
    God's existence;
The repetitively demonstrated progress and "fruits" associated
with belief in and dedication to God;
Man's ability to reason and to create and to innovate, which
separates him from other life and which causes him to
look into and
think into
a higher realm.

If you have received the restored Gospel in its fulness
you can add even more to the "evidence list":
The Book of Mormon, a volume of ancient scripture, covering
a historical period of over a thousand years . . . . so accurate
    and so consistent

with today's archaeology that it cannot be explained or
      accounted for
by anything other than supernatural means.
A church that is growing dramatically as other organized
religions falter and weaken . . . . a church with relevance
rather than obsolescence . . . .
with answers rather than self-contradicting creeds . . . .
A church that changes lives because it is of God and not
      of men . . . .
A church consistent in every way with Christ's Church in the
New Testament . . . . consistent because it *is* His same Church.
Solid *answers* to man's greatest questions . . . . Where did
      I come from?
Why am I here? Where am I going? . . . .
answers that have such reason and beauty that they promote
and foster real faith
(rather than destroying it as do the illogical and seemingly unfair
"answers" of incomplete, man-made philosophies).

Skeptics may judge the evidence inconclusive, but the
      evidence mingles
with the desire and produces faith,
which is the first requirement for successful prayer.

The second requirement is *real intent.*
A child who computes his arithmetic problem and then
asks his father
if his answer is correct
has real intent.
One who asks his father to compute it for him does not.
So it is with our Heavenly Father and with us.
His promise is that He will confirm or disaffirm the answers

we reach . . . . [1]
(through study and the use of our free-agent minds) . . . .
not that He will always furnish us with a ready-made answer of
       His own.
(However, God can and does intercede in situations
where answers are beyond our reach.)
Real intent, in many cases, simply means
work.
So the first two requirements for effective prayer,
are *faith* and *work* . . . (two words that go together well).

The third requirement,
sincerity
so often means so little to us.
We sign our letters with the word, and
we think we recognize the quality by a serious face
and a solemn voice.
Real sincerity goes far beyond these, and is not fully described
unless it is amplified by words like
earnestness,
intensity,
absolute honesty.

Consider one of
the greatest, most *sincere* prayers . . . .
Christ in Gethsemane.
Was it not the Calvary He knew He would face that
made the Gethsemane more intense?
Perhaps our Gethsemanes (prayers) need Calvaries (challenges)

---
[1]Doctrine and Covenants 9:8-9.

to make them sincere.
Many of us who profess faith are quick to acknowledge the
importance of prayer in meeting challenge . . . .
But we forget that the reverse is also true: That it is
the *challenge* at hand that makes the *prayer* successful.
None of us are lacking for challenges . . . . we only fail to
see them and to acknowledge their importance.
Is not the raising of children enough of a Calvary to bring about
some sort of a Gethsemane?
Or how about the filling of a Church calling?
Or the struggle of gaining a strong testimony?
Or the exaltation of your own soul?
Sometimes we subconsciously wait for a Calvary . . . . for
      a challenge
or a crisis . . . .
and we wonder if we will "have what it takes" if we are asked
to give up all for a righteous cause,
or if we are persecuted for our beliefs.
If only we could have the perspective to see
that the toughest challenge is the test of
acceptance,
and affluence,
and apathy,
and noncrisis!
Isn't it true that our most sincere and deepest prayers and
our most profound and genuine humility
come during crisis . . . .
and isn't it true that our most surface and infrequent prayers
happen during times when "all is well" . . . .

and isn't it true that it is hard to get closer to God
at the same time you're getting more accepted by the world?

Surely the greatest challenge is to be consistently humble
and close to God
in times of achievement and accolade.
Contrast the depth of the pioneer's relationship to God
(on whom he depended for survival)
with *our* relationship with God
(whom, in the face of prosperity, we may wonder why we need).
Contrast *your own* prayers on a night when life and death
hang in the balance
with your prayers on a night when all is well.
Clearly, closeness comes with the crisis.
It really should be opposite . . . . for two reasons:
1. We have more to thank God for in a plentiful, crisis-free period.
2. The strength and guidance we receive through noncrisis
       humility
can be used for real contributions
to others
and to God's program
rather than to overcome the crisis that induced it.

One definition of greatness is:
"A man who can be close to God . . . . who can
       communicate earnestly
and deeply
without the presence of some crisis which forces him to do so."

A scriptural way to say the same thing is in this paraphrase
    of Alma:
"More blessed are those who are humble without being compelled
to be humble."[1]

Christ *chose* to have a Calvary . . . . it was not forced on Him.
His choice of it motivated the depth of His Gethsemane
which, in turn,
gave Him the strength to make His Calvary a success.

Many have challenge thrust upon them in the form of a crisis,
but truly great men
choose their challenge . . . . find their cause . . . . .
and sincerely
solicit the Lord's help in that cause.
As a result of their chosen Calvary,
they have their own successful Gethsemane, and their prayers
meet the third requirement of
sincerity.

Learn to thrust down the self-deceptive thought . . . .
    the pride-producing
thought that all things are fine . . . . that you are doing so well
that you can afford to
stop praying,
stop reflecting,
stop studying the Gospel,
stop feeling dependent on God.
The most frequently recurring lesson of the Book of Mormon
is the cycle of

---

[1]Alma 32:12-16.

pride . . . . unrighteousness . . . . . destruction . . . . humility
righteousness . . . . wealth . . . . pride.
Almost every generation had to relearn the same lesson.

True greatness and true capacity to contribute to
        God's kingdom
will result in anyone who can learn this lesson
without taking the time
to experience it.

● With the three requirements of faith, real intent, and sincerity
clearly in your mind . . . .
Ask . . . .
Ask for more help,
Ask for more knowledge,
Ask for stronger testimony,
Ask for more opportunity to serve,
Ask for more help in big decisions and in small things,
Ask for the Spirit of the Holy Ghost,[1]
Ask for knowledge of the truth,[2]
Ask for health and ask to overcome sickness,[3]
Ask for wisdom,[4]
Ask for forgiveness,[5]
Ask to overcome temptation,[6]
Ask to see your foreordained course, and then ask for frequent
course-correction along the way.

The asking and planning are the sharpening of the saw,
and the implementation is the sawing.
Ask daily,[7]
Ask vocally and in your heart,[8]
Ask with great desire . . . . with a *hunger* for an answer.[9]
You will find that the effectual, fervent prayer availeth much;[10]

---

[1]Moroni 10:4-5.
[2]Ibid.
[3]Alma 34:27.
[4]Doctrine and Covenants 6:7.
[5]Alma 34:18.
[6]Doctrine and Covenants 20:33.
[7]Mosiah 4:11.
[8]Doctrine and Covenants 19:28, 38.
[9]Enos 4.
[10]James 5:16.

and that God is anxious to accomplish *His* goal of bringing to
pass the immortality and eternal life of man.[1]
Ask for the capacity to develop the purity and virtue that
will allow your prayers to continue to be answered
and that will produce confidence.[2]
(What a difference there is between man-made "self-confidence"
and God-made confidence in self as a servant and child of God!)

Always preface your asking
with thanksgiving,
for of all people of all time, we have the most
opportunity,
the most knowledge,
the most potential.
Thank Him for your physical body and your mortal opportunity,
Thank Him for the joys of family and of service,
Thank Him for the opportunity to speak with Him.

If you learn best by example, notice that
the scriptures are filled with great prayers:
2 Nephi 4:20-35
Joseph Smith 2
Matthew 6:9-13
Luke 18:10-14
Enos 1-17
Alma 31:12-38
3 Nephi 17

---

[1]Moses 1:39.
[2]Doctrine and Covenants 121:45.

3 Nephi 19
Ether 3
Doctrine and Covenants 121

The most direct way of getting to know anyone is to
Ask and Listen.

Chapter 12

Being and Returning

- "Likes" communicate best.
  The more one has in common with another, the more there is
  to talk about,
  and the more each can give
  to the other.

In most relationships, there is a melting and a fusing
as each grows more like the other . . . .
a gradual meeting at a center-in-between.
In a relationship with God, however,
the movement and the changing must be exclusively with us . . . .
because it is we
who are striving to be
like Him.

Still, just as a master delights in helping a protégé,
so our Father must take joy in our efforts to acquire the perfection
that is His.
Hence, He extends His offer to help . . . .
by asking us to ask.

Any father who has found a measure of joy,
who has unlocked some of the secrets of happiness,
is anxious to somehow transfer them . . . . to pass them on

to his children.
He wants his children to achieve in the areas where he
        has achieved,
to find joy where he has found joy.

God, our Heavenly Father, who has discovered
all joy,
and unlocked all of the secrets,
wants His children to achieve in all areas,
to find all joy,
to be like Him,
to be perfect.[1]

---

[1]Matthew 5:48.

• The first step in being like Him
is to know Him.
(And it is more than just a little step, for "knowing Him"
means "keeping His commandments."[1]
And when you really know someone, you are,
by definition,
quite a bit like him . . . .
thus "knowing Christ"
and "being Christ-like"
are not far removed.

Being Christ-like is a great goal because it is a positive goal.
When you think of being Christ-like,
you think of *being* and *becoming* good things . . . .
(not of *not being* and *avoiding* bad things).
Christ fulfilled Moses' law . . . .
He spoke of what to do, not of what not to do,
and He showed us the higher motivation of the love of good
(rather than the lower motivation of the fear of the consequence
of wrong).
Christ replaced (or reiterated positively) all ten
of the Ten Commandments by giving us
His two commandments of loving God and loving neighbor.

In spite of Christ, and in spite of His positive message,
many "Christians"
feel the deception of self-righteousness. . . . they are not

---

[1] John 2:3-4.

breaking rules
and they are not committing sins of commission . . . .
Yet the Christ-like qualities of charity and compassion may be
far from them,
and they commit the more subtle but no less important sins
of omission.

• The objective of being more like Christ
involves what seems to be a paradox:
If it is true that being more like Him helps us to relate better
to Him,
and if it is also true that relating to Him and communicating with
Him helps us to be more like Him . . . .
then we have a chicken-egg situation . . . .
Which comes first?
Which should we strive for in order to bring about the other?
Should we repent before praying,
or should we pray before repenting?
Answer it with a this-world comparison:
Does the boy know his father better by talking to him
or by trying to be more like him?
The answer, of course is
both.
We pray while we repent, and
we repent while we pray . . . .
In fact,
either is impossible separately.

The statement, ''I have to get my life in order before I can
really ask God for anything,''
is a trap,
for we need His help in order to get our life in order,
and the three requirements for successful prayer are
sincerity, faith, and real intent . . . . three ingredients that
may actually be more evident in a man entering the

repenting process
than in a man who thinks he doesn't need repentance.

On the other hand,
the Lord has said,
"I, the Lord am bound
when ye do what I say;
but when ye do not what I say, ye have no promise."[1]
Thus, the more a man is like Christ, the more effectual
his prayers,
his requests,
his communication,
his relationship with God,
can be.

----

[1]Doctrine and Covenants 82:10.

• The question of how . . . .
how to become more Christ-like . . . .
(how to go about it
and how to think about it)
can be answered many ways.
We will answer it in six different ways here,
and you can see which, if any, of the six
are useful and relevant to you.

1. Let the phrase, "Not mine, but Thy will be done,"[1]
permeate and guide your thoughts and your decisions.
He is like God who does what God would do . . . .
He is like God who does the will of God . . . . and
Perhaps of all prayers, that phrase,
uttered in Gethsemane,
teaches the most.
If you let it become your criteria in all choices,
both big and small,
and if you can be honest enough with yourself to *really* do
what you feel is His will,
then with every choice or decision that you make, you will be more
like Him.
A complete commitment to do His will can
simplify
and clarify
your life by removing all of the many "second-level" criteria
that most men have to deal with
in most decisions.

---

[1]See Luke 22:42.

2. Follow the basic set of priorities that God has revealed.
Place the welfare of your family first,
and the filling of your Church calling next . . . .
both in front of any other objective in any other field.
Again, this can simplify and beautify life
by eliminating the time-consumption and futility of
unequal comparisons.
If a certain move is better for your career but worse for your family,
and if priorities are not well established,
the decision may be a toss-up.
If priorities are clear, the decision will be clear.
If your priorities are His priorities, you are becoming more like Him.

3. View the elements and options of your life
as components of one of three kinds of programs:
God's program,
Satan's program,
Your own program (man's program).
Any alternative involving dishonesty, or cruelty, or retaliation,
or the breaking of any of God's commandments,
is a part of Satan's program.
Any action that involves charity or compassion or love
or the keeping of any of God's commandments
is a part of God's program.
Man sometimes takes the course in between, not breaking
          commandments
but not really living them either . . . .
a "lukewarm" posture that neither achieves nor destroys.
If you have any question about which of the three programs
any particular deed falls into,

magnify the deed by a thousand power . . . . it will then be
easier to identify.
(If you're really not sure whether putting an extra two dollars
on your expense report is part of Satan's program,
magnify it to two thousand dollars, and you'll see that it is.
If you're really not sure that helping a lame man across the street
is part of God's program,
magnify it into, "What ye have done for these, ye have
        done for me,"
and you'll know that it is.)

4. Let the Holy Ghost teach you to be Christ-like.
As discussed earlier,
The Holy Ghost testifies of Christ and teaches of Christ,
and since He is one in purpose with Christ,
His Spirit's presence in our lives make us more like them both.

5. Program yourself by knowing the details and specifics
of Christ's life.
We've all had the experience of reading a particularly good novel,
and identifying so strongly with one of the characters
that we subsequently act a little bit like that character by assuming
some of his traits or some of his views or some of his techniques.
The central character in the greatest story ever told
can do this same thing for us . . . .
if we read that story often enough
and carefully enough,
and prayerfully enough.

6. Work hard at discovering your personal foreordination.
Many elements of becoming Christ-like are the same for every man,
but each individual
has a separate and distinct foreordination . . . .
a particular set of purposes
that Christ would particularly like him to attain.
By discovering and achieving these, we do His will and grow to be
more like Him.
There is no better way to get to know any man
than by getting involved with that man in that man's work . . . .
then you get to know his purposes as well as his methods.
The most meaningful and effective way to be involved in God's
work is to know and complete your own foreordination.

You can find your foreordination by a process of
        "spiritual serendipity."
The word "serendipity," by itself, means a happy accident . . . .
something good, unexpectedly found while seeking
        something else . . . .
found because of sensitivity and observance
and a degree of good fortune.
Add "spiritual" to "serendipity" and it becomes a notion
of divine guidance rather than mere good fortune.
One who seeks direction from the Lord and charts a course
of objectives,
and who then follows that course faithfully, but always
with openness and awareness of other opportunities,
will see the forks in the road and the shortcuts and the
small paths
that lead most directly and most surely to the fulfillment
of foreordination.

• Now, having conceptualized a few ways to go about the process
of "being," we might ask the question:
What direct relationship does "being" have to the other part of this
chapter's title: to returning?
The answer, of course, is that being *is* returning
and returning *is* being.
To all who believe in the reality of a pre-existence with God
and who hope to regain His presence,
the word "return"
has great meaning, and the scriptures tell us that if we
        do return . . . .
if we do see Him again,
we will be like Him.[1]
Thus, returning is being and being is returning.

Peter listed the qualities needed to bring about that return . . . .
the qualities that will assure calling and election and return.
His list was faith,
virtue, knowledge, temperance,
patience, godliness, brotherly kindness, and charity.[2]
Joseph Smith said the same thing on the same topic
in different words:
"Humble yourselves, hunger and thirst after righteousness, live
by every word of God."[3]
Both the ancient apostle and the modern one were telling us
that the way to return
is to be Christ-like.

---

[1] 1 John 3:2.
[2] 2 Peter 1:6-10.
[3] *Teachings of the Prophet Joseph Smith,* p. 150.

● In a relationship with God,
knowing Him,
and loving Him,
and being like Him . . . .
are all synonymous; and the three great admonitions of scripture,
to love God,[1]
to know God,[2]
and to be like God,[3]
are not really three separate admonitions
but one.
"Being" must include "knowing" and "loving."
"Loving" cannot be complete without "being" and "knowing."
"Knowing" is not accurate without "loving" and "being."

The three come about through "asking" and "listening,"
and the three lead to "returning."

---

[1]Matthew 22:37.
[2]John 17:3.
[3]Matthew 5:48.

Index

-A-

Aborigine, 32
Absolutes, 133
Achievement, 5, 130
Act
  learning to, 39
America, 33
Amnesia
  spiritual, 16
Ancestors, 30
Appetites, 31
Apple
  an individual, 149
Appreciation
  sharing, 89
"Ask"
  scriptural admonition, 65, 167, 177
Assumptions
  incorrect, 32
"Aura"
  a human, 48
Auragām
  a game, 55, 57

-B-

Baptism, 154
Blessings
  patriarchal, 36-38
  priesthood, 95
Bodies, 151
Body
  physical, 30, 42
"Book, family interest," 88, 89
Book of Mormon, 170, 171
  recurring lesson of, 175

-C-

Cafe
  watching people from a little, 119
Callings, 34
Calvary, 173, 175
Candor, 124
Challenge, 175
  greatest, 174
Challenges, 32, 173
Charity, 51, 163
Child
  bored, 136
  with an arithmetic problem,
    165, 171
Children, 30, 91, 119-143
  interviews with, 141
  learn from little, 165
  learning to know your, 141, 142
  methods by which they learn,
    132-143
  raising of, 173
  two things we would all want
    to give our, 140
  verbal teaching of, 138
Christ-like, 53, 60, 182
  how to become more, 186
Church, 171
Citizenship, 32
College
  when parents send a child to, 150
Commandments
  Ten, 182
  two, 182
Commitment, 186
Communication, 2, 107, 108
  joy of, 129

Confidence, 20, 21, 126
Country
   your, 32
Covenants
   patriarchal, 96
Create, 66
Creating
   joy of, 130
Creativity, 127
Crisis, 53

-D-

Date
   a weekly, 107
Day
   each, 79
Decisions, 76, 126, 134, 186
"Deed, window," 109
Dependency, 53
Depression, 46
"Description, spouse," 110
Desire, 169, 170
Desires
   parents', 133
Destiny, 16-18, 21, 22
Differences
   basic, between man and woman,
      102-104
Difficulties, 32
Discipline, 18
Discoveries
   sharing, 89

-E-

Earth, 120
   as a laboratory, 73
Emotions, 46-48
Empathy, 109
Enoch, 152
Enos, 168
Environment, 33, 136, 137

Evaluation, 67
Exaltation
   three relationships essential to, 8
Example, 135

-F-

Failure, 130
Faith, 169
   first requirement for successful
      prayer, 171
   the principle of, 18
"Familiarity, first-time," 170
Family, 65, 85, 133
   four pillars of a successful, 87
   love in a, 143
   order of the, 96
   patriarchal order, 96, 97
   sharing, 88
   spirit of the, 91-95
Family home evening
   "executive session" of, 115, 118
Feelings, 108, 129
Field, Henry Martyn, 147
Foreordination
   your personal, 189
Foreordinations, 34
Franklin, Benjamin, 77, 102
Free agency, 17, 59, 72
Freedom, 32
   joy of, 126
Fulfillment, 65
Future, 66
   plans for the, 77

-G-

"Game, out-giving," 109
Gap
   between where you are and where
      you should be, 37
Gethsemane, 172, 173, 186

Gift
  each person is given a, 29
Gifts
  six categories of, 29
Giving, 50, 51
Goals
  achievement, 69, 70
  family, 130
  four principles in setting, 114, 115
  lifetime, 113
  on a yearly basis, 113
  pursuit of, 75
  relationship, 69, 70
  review, 76
God
  child of, 26, 27
  criteria for knowing, 159-161
  evidence of, 170
  handiwork of, 19
  our spirit Father, 149
  pioneer's relationship to, 174
  returning to, 190
  service to, 61
  spirit children of, 17
  testimony of, 157
Godhead, 152, 153
Golden rule, 49
Gospel, 154
  central purpose of the, 149
  distribution of the truths of the, 61
  full confidence in the, 94
Greatness, one definition of, 174

-H-

Happiness, 64
  measurement of, 3
Harvest
  law of the, 129
Holy Ghost, 21, 53, 152, 188
  how to get the Spirit of the, 92
  joy of feeling the, 125
  presence of the, 79
  Spirit of the, 91, 137

Home, 85, 92, 126
  Gospel, 139
  when you are, 93
Honesty, 124
Humility, 19, 20
Humor
  joy of a sense of, 128
Husband, 26

-I-

Identity, 16-18, 21, 22
  family, 99, 128
Imagination, 127
Imperfection
  human, 131
I.Q.
  differences in, 136
Intelligences, 17
Interview
  approaching an, 164

-J-

Jehovah, 150
Jesus Christ
  being more like, 184
  Gospel of, 33
  in Gethsemane, 172
  relationship to, 22
  to know, 153
Journal, 78
Joy, 180, 181
  source of real, 101
Joys, 58, 122, 123, 132

-K-

Kingdom, prerequisites to enter the
  celestial, 52
Knowledge, 21, 138
  earthly, 155

-L-

Law, 133
  natural, 152
  obedience to, 129
Laws, 134
  parents', 133
Learn
  teaching children *how to*, 136
Lee, President Harold B., 86
Liberty, 33
Life, 18, 64, 72
  objectives of, 22
  three kinds of programs in, 187
"Likes," 180
Listening, 50, 107
  joy of, 128
Living
  joy of, 125
Locations, 36
Locomotive
  on a seventy-mile night journey, 114
Love, 125
  joy of man-woman, 129
Lucifer, 150

-M-

McKay, President David O., 86
Man
  on a train, 16
Map, 36
  topographical relief, 37
Marriage
  how to achieve oneness in, 106-117
  institution of, 102
  specialization in, 103
Mind, 45
  unstimulated, 44
Mirrors, 49
Moods
  "lightning," 47
  two effective 46, 37
  "waves," 47
Mortality, 44

Mother, 104
  difference in, 136, 137
Motivation, 182
Muscle, 45

-N-

"Need," 8
Needs, 111
Neighbors, 30

-O-

Objectives
  specific, 67
Observations
  sharing, 88, 89
Occupation
  Church service and, 61-63
Oneness, 104, 113
Opportunities, 31
Origins
  16-18, 21, 22
Orphan
  who discovers that he is the son
    of the King, 20
Out-giving, 109

-P-

Pain, 32
Passersby
  adult, 119
Passions, 31
Paul, 168
Perfection, 36, 60
  our efforts to acquire, 180
  system of, 77, 78
Persistence, 167, 168
Peter, 52, 190
Plan, 75
Planning, 79
Pond
  beaver, 35
Possessions
  worldly, 31

Potentials, 31
Prayer, 79, 94, 165, 177
    family, 125
    three essential elements in
        successful, 169
Prayers, 154
    contrast in our, 174
    great, 178, 179
Pre-existence, 17, 22, 59, 149
"Pride, family," 99
Priesthood
    His, 33
    if you hold the, 95
    role of the, 97
    using the, 125
Principles
    correct, 126
Priorities
    basic set of, 187
Priority
    first, 65, 85
Progression
    eternal, 18, 36
Projects
    family, 127
Prophecy, 170
Prophets
    school of the, 94
Psychiatry, 20
Psychology, 20
Purpose, 113
    our, 16-18, 21, 22

                -Q-
Quarreling, 93
Quarrels, 125
Questions
    when children ask, 138

                -R-
Real intent
    requirement for successful
        prayer, 171

Realness, 124
Reason
    man's ability to, 170
Receiving, 50, 51
Receptivity
    total, 124
Re-evaluation, 67
"Relating"
    two forms of, 5
Relationship
    components of an ideal, 6, 160,
        161
Relationships
    real, 8
Remorse, 46
Repentance, 184, 185
Reputation
    good, 126
Responsibilities, 34
Rogers, Karl, 107

                -S-
Sacrament, 154
Scriptures, 36, 155, 170, 188
Security, 113
    joy of, 126
Self-deception, 175
Self-image, 55, 111
Senses
    five, 42, 43
"Serendipity," 189
Service
    joy of, 131
Sharing, 88, 89
    joy of, 128
Sincerity
    requirement for successful prayer,
        172
Singleness, 102
Sleep
    resolve discontent before, 93
Smith, Joseph, 190
Social skills, 49-51

Spirituality, 52-54
Stars, 19
Stewardship, 29-34, 119
  responsibility of, 121
  reward of, 121
  two-way, 29, 30
Stimulation
  environment of, 136
Strengths, 66
Success, 86
Sun, 19
Sunday
  what to do on, 76, 77
"Synergysm," 104

-T-

"Table, family round," 89
Teaching, 139
Teachings
  Gospel's, 36
Temptation, 53
Testimony, 130, 157
Thanksgiving, 178
Things, 5
  place for, 97
Time, 72
  individual, 141
  misused, 74
  segmented, 73
  three kinds of, 73
  unused, 74
  well-used, 74
Tone, 139

Tool
  well-maintained, 43
Traditions
  family, 99
Train
  man on a, 16
Trust
  child's, 125
  God's greatest, 30
Truth, 126
  Gospel, 155

-U-

Understanding, 131
Uniqueness, 38
Unity, 98
Universe, 170

-W-

Walks
  long, 2
"Wall, family-favorite-things," 89
Wealth, 61
Wells, H. G., 147
Wife, 104
  role of the, 97
Windows, 49
Work, 172
  joy of hard, 127
  most important, 86
World
  today's, 65